D0608037

This book is for my mother and my grandmothers, who encouraged my interest in cooking.

BRUNCH — THE ELEGANT AND ECONOMICAL WAY TO ENTERTAIN

Brunches are a fun, elegant and economical way to entertain. They make for a memorable occasion and beat the cost of dinner parties ten (dollars) to one. This book is the answer to serving a perfect Brunch everytime.

- This book begins with a list of menu ideas for nine special occasions, including A Mother's Day Brunch, An Easter Brunch, A Trim-the-Tree Brunch and more (see page 5).
- Preparation Pointers are included to help you avoid last-minute flurries and ensure that things go smoothly.
- Beautiful full-color photographs show you how the recipes look when they are prepared.
- As with all Nitty Gritty Cookbooks, the recipes are easy to follow and are printed one per page in large, easy-to-read type.
- For added convenience, this book is uniquely designed to take a minimum of counter space and to keep your place when folded open.

SATISFACTION GUARANTEE—If you are not completely satisfied with any Nitty Gritty book, we will gladly refund your purchase price. Simply return it to us within 30 days along with your receipt.

Meet the Author

A member of the International Association of Cooking Schools, Christie Williams has been teaching cooking lessons for over five years. Recently she completed the advanced course series at the Cordon Bleu in London.

Her first two cookbooks, **What's Cookin'** and **What's Cookin' 2**, contain recipes created especially for the food processor.

Christie lives in Federal Way, Washington with her husband and eight year old son, Darrin.

Brunch

by Christie Williams

photographs by Glen Millward
illustrations by Mike Nelson

A Nitty Gritty Book*
Published by
Nitty Gritty Productions
P.O. Box 5457
Concord, California 94524

*Nitty Gritty Books—Trademark
Owned by Nitty Gritty Productions
Concord, California

Printed in the U.S.A.
by Mariposa Press
Concord, California
Edited by Maureen Reynolds

ISBN 0-911954-59-7
Library of Congress Catalog Card Number: 80-85004

Table of Contents

Introduction

There's no doubt about it, brunches are gaining in popularity. Brunches offer one of the most versatile forms of entertaining ever. They can be quick, easy and casual or formal, elegant and sophisticated. The assortment of foods that can be served at a brunch is practically endless. From simple scrambled eggs and bacon with store-bought sweet rolls to an elaborate layered Crêpe Gâteau and homemade Almond Danish. In this day of rising food costs, brunches beat steak dinners ten (dollars) to one. Many of the dishes can be prepared ahead, allowing the host and hostess to enjoy the party as much as their guests.

Brunches celebrate almost anything-Mother's Day, Father's Day holidays, showers, graduations OR after-the-tennis-match.

The number of guests invited and the time of the brunch are flexible, but be sure to keep the number manageable. The usual starting time for a brunch is around 11 a.m., but an hour either way is perfectly acceptable.

So many husbands and wives work full-time nowadays that the weekend is the only time for a leisurely brunch and change of pace, a chance to wind down from a hectic week and enjoy family and friends. And lingering over that last cup of coffee is a good way to catch up with each other.

Preparation Pointers

One of the nicest things about a brunch is that so much of the preparation can be done ahead of time, leaving the hostess free to enjoy her guests. Advance preparation and organization prevents last-minute flurries. Keep in mind that not ALL of the dishes served need be complicated nor made from scratch. Special bakeries, delicatessens and gourmet food centers offer delectable items to choose from. Don't hesitate to purchase freshly made croissants, bagels or donuts to round out your menu. An assortment of special cheeses or spicy sausages might be just the thing to complement your quiche or casserole.

It's important to have a timetable in mind and tailor your schedule to allow advance preparation or partial preparation. Read each recipe carefully and make sure you un-

derstand each step. Try to envision the finished product. Estimate the preparation time. Keep your cooking utensils and appliances in mind: make sure you don't have two dishes that require baking at different temperatures if you have only one oven. Make sure you have ample refrigerator space. A pre-assembled casserole, several bottles of wine and eight fruit cups can take up a lot of space! Set the table or arrange your buffet the night before. Have serving dishes and utensils ready. Make a list of the cooking times of each dish you are serving. Working backwards from your scheduled serving time, decide when you should start the first dish and proceed accordingly. Careful planning helps assure a success.

Menu Planning

A successful menu requires forethought. Keep in mind seasonal specials and take advantage of fresh vegetables, fruits and berries. A variety of textures, tastes, colors and shapes should be included. The proper balance of hot and cold, crisp and soft, bland and tart, sweet and spicy, all add interest and contrast to your meal. For example, the Melon, Cucumber and Tomato Salad would be a good dish to serve with Klara's Crab Quiche. The quiche is hot, rich and yellow-colored, while the salad is cold, its ingredients are chopped and it contains the colors green and red.

Attractive garnishes and imaginative presentation show that the cook has taken time to please the eye as well as the palate. Many times I have received compliments on my pies, not only because they taste great, but because I baked them in a rectangular instead of the traditional pie pan. So, take an extra minute and float a lemon slice in each glass of water; learn how to fold napkins in interesting ways; warm your plates in the oven, and demonstrate in small but important details the full art of entertaining.

MENU IDEAS

An Omelet Brunch
Bloody Marys, p. 33
Sausage Cheese Balls, p. 13
Make Your Own Omelet, p. 52
Hot and Cold Fillings, p. 54, 55
Brandied Fresh Fruit, p. 36
Kentucky Butter Cake, p. 172

A Trim-the-Tree Brunch
Champagne and Orange Juice
Brandied Camembert, p. 10
Fantastic Mushroom Eggs with
    Cheese and Cream Sauce, p. 60
Sausage Ring, p. 88
Pumpkin Muffins, p. 103
Hot Buttered Cranberry Punch, p. 28
Christmas Cookies, Fruit Cake

A Father's Day Brunch
1-2-3 Frozen Daiquiris, p. 27
Crab-Stuffed Mushrooms, p. 17
Fresh Pan-Fried Trout, p. 79
Hash Browns
Sunnyside-Up Eggs
Sliced Ripe Tomatoes
Crumbly Walnut Coffee Cake, p. 132

A Mother's Day Brunch
Strawberry Daiquiris, p. 26
Bacon-Wrapped Tidbits, p. 12
Easy Baked Eggs, p. 78
Sliced Ham
Rum-Baked Fruit, p. 41
Almond Danish, p. 138

A Fall Saturday Family Breakfast
Cocoa Mocha, p. 29
Scrambled Eggs
Corn Fritters, Maple Syrup, p. 93
Link Sausage
Baked Apples with Cream

A Pack-Along Boating or Picnic Brunch
White Wine, Coffee
Avocado-Stuffed Eggs/Chinese Tea Eggs,
    pgs. 18 and 19
Sausages in a Pastry Shell, p. 89
Assorted Mustards
Copper Pennies, p. 159
Fresh Fruit
Sour Cream Poppy Seed Cake, p. 167

Easter Brunch
Slush, p. 30
Cheese Krispies, p. 8
Stuffed Cherry Tomatoes, p. 14
Tangy Raspberry Soup, p. 47
Ham and Shrimp Gâteau, p. 120
Cottage Cheese Croissants, p. 142
Rum Mousse Pie, p. 171

An Italian Style Brunch
Kir
Mushrooms in Garlic, p. 9
Zucchini Quiche with Cheese Crust, p. 70
Italian Sausage
Melon with Port
Crusty Rolls, Butter
Cheese Ice Cream, p. 162

A Summer Brunch
German Fruit Bowle, p. 24
Savory Chicken Tart, p. 84
Fresh Vegetable Frittata, p. 82
Broiled Tomatoes, p. 95
Brown Sugar Sticky Buns, p. 140
Creamy Orange Fondue, p. 164

Note: Recipes without page numbers are not found in this cookbook.

5

Appetizers

Appetizers should be just that—a bit of food to entice the appetite and make guests look forward to things to come. In all likelihood, brunch guests have not eaten since the evening before and will appreciate something to nibble on. If you are serving an alcoholic beverage, be sure to keep it on the light side when people are famished.

If you seem to be running out of ideas for appetizers, don't forget that quiches (leftover or fresh) can be cut into small wedges or squares and served as appetizers. Weight watchers will appreciate a selection of crudities (finger-sized portions of fresh vegetables) to nibble on. A low-calorie dip would also be nice to have on hand.

In order that your brunch runs smoothly, all the appetizers in this chapter can be made in advance. Another handy item to have is an electric warming tray. It can be used for appetizers as well as rolls, vegetables and main dishes.

Appetizers seem to have a way of getting people to circulate and visit, don't neglect them.

Cheese Krispies

1 cup grated sharp Cheddar cheese
1/2 cup butter, softened
1 cup all-purpose flour
1/2 tsp. salt
1 tsp. red pepper
1 cup Rice Krispies cereal

   Combine cheese and butter in a mixing bowl. Mash together until well combined. Stir in flour, salt and red pepper. Add Rice Krispies and mix thoroughly. Dough may be refrigerated or frozen at this point if desired.* Drop by teaspoonfuls (1-inch apart) onto an unbuttered cookie sheet. Flatten slightly with a fork. Bake at 350°F. for 12 minutes. Makes 6 dozen.
   *Refrigerate for up to 10 days in advance. Freeze for up to 1 month.

Mushrooms In Garlic Butter

This recipe is similar to those used for escargot. Be sure to make plenty because people who are timid about eating snails are bold when it comes to these mushrooms!

2 dozen large fresh mushrooms
   (about 1 1/2 inches in diameter)
1/2 cup butter
2 cloves garlic, minced
2 shallots, minced

1/2 cup minced parsley
1/2 tsp. fresh lemon juice
1/2 tsp. salt
1/4 tsp. pepper

Wipe or rinse mushrooms clean and remove stems. Discard stems or save them for another use. Combine butter, garlic, shallots and parsley in the workbowl of a food processor or in small mixing bowl. Process or mix until combined. Add lemon juice, salt and pepper. Blend briefly. Place mushrooms in a shallow baking dish. Fill each mushroom cap with a dollop of the garlic butter mixture (about 1/2 or 1 tsp.). Bake at 400°F. for 10 to 12 minutes, or until bubbly. Serve with crusty French bread, if desired. Use toothpicks to spear the mushrooms. Urge guests to dip bread into the remaining butter. Provide small plates and plenty of napkins. Makes 6 to 8 appetizer servings.

Brandied Camembert

This very elegant appetizer should be prepared at least 24 hours in advance to allow the flavors to mellow. Serve with very plain crackers or wedges of unpeeled fresh apples or pears. If you want to slice the apples or pears in advance, sprinkle each slice with a little fresh lemon juice. Store in plastic wrap up to 6 hours.

This can also be served as a European-style dessert, and Brandied Camembert makes a nice gift from your kitchen around holiday time.

1 pkg. (8 ozs.) Camembert cheese
1/2 cup butter
2 tbs. brandy
1/2 cup sliced almonds, toasted (see page 14, for toasting instructions)

Remove rind from Camembert and discard. Cut cheese and butter into 1-inch cubes. Using a food processor or electric mixer, combine Camembert, butter and brandy until thoroughly blended. Shape mixture into a ball, using plastic wrap (this will keep fingers from sticking). Press toasted almonds over the surface. Wrap tightly and refrigerate. Remove from the refrigerator 20 minutes before serving. Makes 2 cheese balls.

Hot Cream Cheese Dip

This delicious dip is easily assembled in a food processor.

1 pkg. (8 ozs.) cream cheese
1 cup sour cream
1 medium-sized green pepper
   (diced, if not using processor)
4 green onions
   (diced, if not using processor)

1 pkg (8 ozs.) dried beef,
   coarsely chopped
dash of Tabasco sauce
1/2 tsp. EACH salt and pepper
1/2 cup chopped walnuts
assorted crackers

Cut the cream cheese into chunks and place in work bowl of food processor or a large mixing bowl. Add sour cream. Process or beat until smooth. If using processor, seed green pepper and slice green onion into 2-inch lengths. Add green pepper, green onions, dried beef and seasonings to cream cheese mixture. Process, using on/off turns, or beat briefly until ingredients are well blended. Place in a shallow ovenproof casserole. Sprinkle nuts on top. Bake at 350°F. for 15 minutes. Serve hot with assorted crackers.

Bacon-Wrapped Tidbits

Any number of tidbits can be wrapped in a small slice of bacon, skewered with a wooden toothpick and broiled until the bacon is crisp.

1/2 lb. bacon strips, cut into thirds
36 ''tidbits''
toothpicks
''Tidbit'' suggestions: pitted dates, whole waterchestnuts, pineapple chunks, banana chunks, large mushrooms, small oysters, chicken livers (cut in half: marinate in soy sauce overnight), pitted green olives, large shrimp (shelled and deveined.)

Wrap bacon around tidbit and secure with a toothpick. Place in a shallow baking pan. Broil 6 inches from the heat until bacon is crisp, turning once. Oysters, chicken livers and shrimp must be cooked through. Serve hot. Makes 36.

Sausage Cheese Balls

These easy-to-make appetizers go well with egg dishes. Sausage Cheese Balls can be made ahead and frozen for up to a month.

1 pkg. (12 ozs.) hot bulk sausage
1 lb. sharp Cheddar cheese, shredded
1 cup biscuit mix
For dipping (optional) hot mustards
catsup mixed with horseradish

Mix uncooked sausage, cheese and biscuit mix until thoroughly combined. Shape into walnut-sized balls. Crumple a large sheet of foil. Smooth out and place on a baking sheet. This allows excess fat to drip away from the Sausage Cheese Balls and collect in the creases. Place balls on top of foil about 1 inch apart (may be frozen at this point). Bake at 350°F. for 35 to 45 minutes, or until golden brown. Serve hot. Makes 4 dozen.

Cherry Cream Cheese Spread

This unusual combination will delight your guests. The flavor of most nuts is enhanced by toasting. Spread them in a single layer on a cookie sheet. Bake at 350°F. for 10 to 15 minutes, stirring occasionally until golden.

1 cup pitted Bing cherries (frozen or canned), thoroughly drained
1/2 cup Grand Marnier liqueur
2 pkgs. (8 ozs. each) cream cheese
1 cup chopped toasted almonds
mild-flavored crackers

Cover cherries with liqueur and refrigerate for 24 hours. Drain and discard liqueur. Beat cream cheese with an electric mixer until fluffy. By hand, stir in cherries and almonds. Using plastic wrap, shape mixture into a ball or log. Wrap and store in the refrigerator.* Serve with crackers. Makes 1 ball or log.
    *Keeps well for up to two weeks.

Stuffed Cherry Tomatoes

Cherry tomatoes seem to be a natural when it comes to appetizers. Try filling them with one of the following:

36 cherry tomatoes

Filling Suggestions:
- smoked oysters
- guacamole
- mayonnaise mixed with crumbled, cooked bacon and chopped green onions
- cream cheese mixed with smoked salmon, chopped chives and Worcestershire sauce

Wash and stem cherry tomatoes. Hollow centers with a serrated grapefruit spoon. Turn tomatoes upside down on paper towels to drain for about 15 minutes. Fill with desired filling. Chill for 15 minutes. Serve. Makes 36.

Seafood Mousse

Whether you use shrimp, crab or lobster, this mousse is delicious. Make it the day before so the flavors have a chance to mellow.

1 pkg. unflavored gelatin
1/4 cup cold water
1 can (10 ozs.) tomato soup, undiluted
1 pkg (8 ozs.) cream cheese
1/2 cup finely chopped celery
1/2 cup finely chopped green onions
1/2 cup finely chopped green pepper

1 cup shrimp, crab, or lobster
1 cup mayonnaise
1 tsp. Worcestershire sauce
1 tsp. salt
1/2 tsp. pepper
dash of Tabasco sauce

Dissolve gelatin in cold water. Place soup in saucepan over medium heat. Cut cream cheese into cubes and stir into soup until blended. Add gelatin and stir thoroughly. Remove from heat and combine with remaining ingredients. Pour into a well-oiled 6-cup mold. Cover and refrigerate at least 12 hours. To unmold, dip mold into hot water for several seconds. This will loosen mousse and allow it to unmold more easily. Serve on a platter lined with lettuce leaves and surrounded by crackers.

Crab-Stuffed Mushrooms

These savory morsels make a good beginning for a brunch featuring an asparagus and Cheddar quiche, Canadian bacon, Fresh Fruit Compote, champagne and a gooey dessert.

3/4 pound large mushrooms
1 pkg. (8 ozs.) cream cheese
1/2 cup finely crushed croutons
1/4 tsp. garlic powder

1/2 pound crab meat
2 tbs. grated Parmesan cheese
paprika

Wipe or rinse mushrooms clean and remove stems. Discard stems or save them for another use. Mix cream cheese with crushed croutons and garlic powder until fluffy. Pick over crab meat, removing all cartilage. Stir into cream cheese mixture. Place mushrooms on a baking sheet. Place a spoonful of the crab mixture in the center of each, mounding slightly. Sprinkle with Parmesan and dust with paprika. Broil until piping hot, about 5 minutes. Watch carefully so they don't burn. Makes 8 appetizer servings.

Avocado-Stuffed Eggs

For an extra special effect, spoon the filling into a pastry bag and pipe it decoratively into the eggs.

12 hard-cooked eggs
1 small, ripe avocado, peeled and seeded
1/2 tsp. garlic salt
1/2 tsp. dry mustard
1/2 tsp. EACH salt and pepper
1 tsp. mayonnaise

Cut each egg in half lengthwise. Remove yolks and combine with avocado, beating until light and fluffy. Add garlic salt, dry mustard, salt, pepper and mayonnaise. Beat until smooth. Fill eggs with mixture, using a pastry bag or a spoon. Dust the tops with cayenne (if you like spicy eggs) or paprika. Garnish with parsley. Refrigerate until serving time. Makes 24.

Chinese Tea Eggs

Different, easy and good. These eggs would be nice to serve with Bloody Marys as an appetizer for a brunch featuring Crab Florentine Casserole as the main dish. Because these eggs need to marinate for 24 to 48 hours, they are ideal for advance preparation.

12 eggs
6 tea bags
4 cups water

1/2 cup salt
1/2 cup soy sauce
1/2 cup mayonnaise

Place eggs in a large saucepan, cover with water and bring to a boil over high heat. Cover pan and remove from heat. Let eggs stand 15 minutes, then run under cold water to stop cooking. Gently tap each egg with a spoon to crack entire surface of shell. DO NOT remove shells. Prepare marinade by placing tea bags, 4 cups water, salt and soy in a saucepan. Bring to a boil. Pour over eggs. Cover and refrigerate for 24 to 48 hours. To serve, discard marinade and shell eggs. Cut in half lengthwise and garnish with a dollop of mayonnaise. Makes 24.

Brie En Croûte

This spectacular appetizer freezes beautifully and is SO delicious. Each round croûte should serve 2 to 4 people. Adding a pinch of salt to the egg makes the glaze spread more evenly.

1 pkg. frozen patty shells, thawed
3 small rounds Brie cheese
1 egg
pinch of salt

Roll out each patty shell on a lightly floured board into a circle measuring 5 1/2 inches in diameter. Place 1 Brie round in center of one patty round. Fold up sides. Cut a circle in a second pastry round using the empty Brie can as a guide. Place this round on top of Brie. Cut the edges of the circle in two. Use these pastry strips to seal edges of the pastry-wrapped cheese. In a small bowl beat egg with a fork, adding a pinch of salt. Brush entire bundle with egg, making sure edges of crust are sealed tightly around cheese. Repeat procedure with remaining cheeses.* Bake on a lightly buttered cookie sheet in a preheated

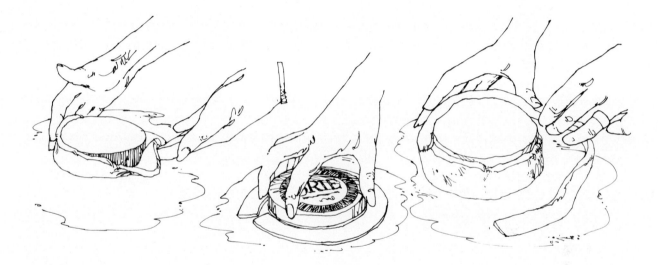

450°F. oven for 15 minutes. Turn oven to 350°F. and continue baking for 20 minutes longer, or until puffed and golden. Cut into wedges. Serve with crackers or fruit.

    *Can be frozen at this point for up to 2 months.

Beverages

Steaming cups of freshly perked coffee or bracing hot tea are a must at any brunch. In the winter, a hot punch or liqueur-laced coffees are particularly appealing. In the spring and summer, lighter sparkling drinks are in order.

Whatever beverage you serve, make sure to keep hot drinks hot and cold drinks cold. Garnishes are easy and effective when it comes to serving beverages. Make a pretty ice ring for punches by pouring water over sliced citrus fruits, fresh berries and bright green leaves in a ring mold. Simply freeze solid and unmold into the punch bowl when ready to serve. Frosting glasses is easy, too: dip the rim of each glass into water or lemon juice and then into sugar. Place glasses in the freezer briefly to frost. A cinnamon stick makes a good swizzle stick for hot chocolate, mulled cider or spiced wine.

Beverages are shown clockwise, outer to inner, beginning in upper left corner: Pina Colada, p. 33; champagne; Salty Dog, p. 33; Mint Julep, p. 33; Cocoa Mocha, p. 29; Mexican Coffee, p. 32; Strawberry Daiquiri, p. 26; Bloody Mary, p. 33.

German Fruit Bowle

When I visited friends in Germany in the summer of 1980, they made this festive fruit drink. They were happy to share the recipe when I asked for it for my Brunch Cookbook.

2 pints fresh strawberries
1 cup sugar
1 bottle Rhine wine
2 bottles Champagne

Wash, hull and cut the strawberries into 1/4-inch cubes. Place in a deep glass bowl and sprinkle with sugar. Pour in wine and stir. Cover bowl and let fruit marinate in wine overnight. To serve, place 1/4 cup of fruit and wine mixture in a pretty goblet, fill to the top with ice-cold champagne. Serves 8 to 12.

Variation: replace strawberries with 2 cups peeled, seeded and diced peaches.

Coffee Pot Punch

This spicy hot punch is perfect for a winter brunch. Pumpkin Cake with Cream Cheese Frosting goes well with this drink.

1 1/2 quarts cranberry juice
2 quarts apple juice
1/2 cup firmly packed brown sugar
1/2 tsp. salt
4 cinnamon sticks
1 1/2 tsp. ground cloves

Pour juices into a 30-cup percolator. Place sugar and spices in the basket. Place basket in the pot and perk. Serve hot in mugs. Serves 12 with enough for seconds.

Strawberry Daiquiris

I am quite certain that this is the best Strawberry Daiquiri ever! Cream of coconut is very sweet, you may wish to use less, taste as you blend. Cream of coconut is usually available in the mixer or liquor section of most supermarkets.

1 pkg. (16 ozs.) frozen, whole, unsweetened strawberries
1 cup cream of coconut (or less)
1/4 cup fresh lemon juice
1/4 cup grenadine syrup
1 to 1 1/2 cups rum

Combine all ingredients in a food processor or blender. Process or blend until smooth. Serves 4.

1-2-3 Frozen Daiquiris

It's easy to memorize this recipe!

1 can (6 ozs.) frozen limeade concentrate, defrosted
2 cans (6 ozs.) full of white rum
3 cans (6 ozs.) full of water
dash of green food coloring, if desired.

Stir all ingredients together. Place in covered container and store in freezer for 5 hours, or overnight. To serve, break up mixture with a spoon and scoop into champagne glasses. Serves 8.

Hot Buttered Cranberry Punch

Have a "Trim the Tree Brunch." Serve this punch with an assortment of Christmas cookies and fruit cake for dessert.

1 can (16 ozs.) jellied cranberry sauce
1/3 cup firmly packed brown sugar
1/4 tsp. cinnamon
1/4 tsp. allspice
1/8 tsp. cloves

1/8 tsp. nutmeg
1/8 tsp. salt
2 cups water
2 cups unsweetened pineapple juice
butter pats, for serving

Combine all ingredients except butter pats in a large saucepan. Stir over medium heat until cranberry sauce is melted. Reduce heat to simmer and cook gently for 2 hours. To serve, ladle into mugs and float a pat of butter on top of each. Serves 8 to 10.

Cocoa Mocha

This mix keeps for up to one week in the refrigerator.

1 can (15 ozs.) sweetened condensed milk
1 bar (4 ozs.) German sweet chocolate, melted
1 cup whipping cream, whipped

Melt chocolate with condensed milk in the top of a double boiler over low heat. Stir occasionally. Cool. Fold whipped cream into cooled chocolate mixture.

To serve: put 1/4 cup of mixture into a mug. Fill to the top with hot coffee. Stir and serve. Store any remaining mixture covered in the refrigerator. Makes 12 servings.

Slush

This fruit drink is light and refreshing and very easily prepared ahead of time. An orange slice skewered together with a cherry makes an effective garnish.

2 cups sugar
9 cups water
1 can (12 ozs.) frozen orange juice
concentrate, undiluted
1 can (12 ozs.) frozen lemonade
concentrate, undiluted
2 cups gin or vodka
1 quart 7-Up OR Squirt, carbonated beverage

Combine sugar and water in a saucepan. Bring to a boil. Reduce heat and simmer 15 minutes. Remove from heat. Add juice concentrates and gin. Pour into a covered container and freeze for several hours or overnight. To serve, fill glass half full of Slush mixture, fill to the top with 7-Up. Makes 2 1/2 quarts. Slush mixture can remain frozen for up to 2 months.

Fruit Julius

Select the fruits of your choice for a variety of flavors.

Choose ONE:
    3 ozs. frozen orange juice concentrate, undiluted
    1 medium sized banana, cubed
    6 ozs. frozen strawberries, thawed
    6 ozs. frozen peaches, thawed
5 to 6 ice cubes
1/2 cup milk
1/2 cup water
1/4 cup sugar
1 tbs. vanilla instant breakfast powder
    or vanilla instant pudding mix, dry

Mix all ingredients together in a blender or food processor. Serves 2.

Fancy Coffees

The following recipes will give you some ideas for turning ordinary coffee into something sublime.

For EACH serving: place 6 ounces of fresh hot coffee in a mug. Add 1 teaspoon of brown sugar and the liqueur of your choice. Top with whipped cream.

SPANISH COFFEE—add 1 ounce EACH Kahlua and rum

AMARETTO COFFEE—2 ounces Amaretto

COFFEE NUDGE—1 ounce EACH Kahlua, brandy and creme de cacao

GRASSHOPPER COFFEE—1 ounce EACH creme de menthe and white creme de cacao

COFFEE ALEXANDER—1 ounce EACH brandy and creme de cacao

COFFEE VELVET—1 ounce EACH creme de cacao and triple sec. Garnish with a pinch of nutmeg and a slice of orange

IRISH COFFEE—2 ounces Irish whisky

A HAPPY MARRIAGE—2 ounces brandy and 1 tbs. instant pre-sweetened cocoa mix

MEXICAN COFFEE—1 ounce Tia Maria and 1 ounce creme de cacao

Quick Ideas for Cold Drinks

Apricot Delight In a glass filled with ice, pour 1 jigger of vodka. Fill remainder of glass with equal parts apricot nectar and 7-Up. Stir.

Bloody Mary In a glass filled with ice, pour 1 to 2 jiggers of vodka. Add 2 to 3 drops Tabasco sauce, dash of Worcestershire sauce, celery salt and pepper to taste. Fill remainder of glass with tomato juice. Stir. Garnish with a celery stalk.

Champagne Mimosa Equal parts chilled champagne and orange juice.

Mint Julep Crush 3 sprigs of fresh mint in the bottom of a highball glass. Add 1 teaspoon of sugar. Fill glass with crushed ice. Add 2 to 3 ounces of bourbon. Stir until disolved. Store in freezer until serving time (at least 20 minutes). Garnish with another sprig of mint.

Piña Colada Stir together 1 ounce cream of coconut, 2 ounces pineapple juice and 1 1/2 ounces rum. Pour in a glass filled with crushed ice. Garnish with a pineapple spear.

Salty Dog Dip the rim of a glass in fresh lemon juice. Roll in salt. Add ice. Pour in 1 to 2 ounces vodka. Fill remainder of glass with grapefruit juice.

Wine Spritzers Fill a wine glass with equal parts white wine and 7-Up.

Tropical Delight Fill a champagne glass with equal parts guava juice and champagne.

Fruit

I am a firm believer that every brunch should offer fruit in one form or another. A beautiful bowl heaped with plump, juicy fruit is decorative and tempting. Use it as a centerpiece and then at dessert time offer crisp crackers and an assortment of cheeses, or pass a platter of irresistible cookies.

Try something just a little bit different—a chilled fruit soup. Serve it in tall, frosted glasses to sip; or serve it in your loveliest tea cups as a prelude to your summer brunch.

When fall chills the air, hot baked fruit is just the thing to enliven your brunch. Most of the fruit recipes offered in this section can also be served as the dessert course.

Brandied Fresh Fruit

This recipe calls for your loveliest glass bowl.

1 can (6 ozs.) frozen orange juice concentrate, thawed
1/2 cup brandy
2 pints fresh strawberries
8 fresh peaches
sugar, to taste

Stir together orange juice and brandy. Wash and hull strawberries, leaving them whole. Peel (see page 48), seed and slice peaches. Place fruit in bowl, sprinkle with sugar. Pour orange juice mixture over. Stir gently to combine. Cover and refrigerate for several hours. Stir once or twice while mixture is mellowing. Serves 8.

Cherries Escoffier

I picked up this handy recipe while at the Cordon Bleu cooking school in London. It's an extremely useful and deliciously flavored sauce. Use it for topping crêpes, ice cream, or as a sauce for roast duck or chicken.

1 lb. fresh Bing cherries
1/8 tsp. cinnamon
2 tbs. sugar
1 orange
1/2 cup red burgundy wine
4 tbs. red currant jelly, lightly beaten

Pit cherries. Place in a saucepan with cinnamon and sugar. Cover and cook slowly for 5 minutes ONLY, over medium-low heat. Do not add water; cherries should burst and run with juice. Meanwhile, grate entire orange and squeeze all the juice from it. Combine orange rind and juice with wine in another saucepan. Cook over medium heat until amount from it is reduced by half. Add beaten currant jelly to mixture. When jelly has melted into wine mixture, add to cherries. Serve warm or cool. Makes 4 cups.

Fresh Strawberries With Grand Marnier

The combination of juicy ripe strawberries and zesty orange, along with the rich liqueur, makes a delightful dish all by itself. However, it can be used as a topping for ice cream or crêpes as well.

2 pint baskets fresh strawberries
1/4 to 1/3 cup sugar (to taste)
1/2 cup Grand Marnier liqueur
grated peel of one orange

Wash and stem strawberries. Use slicing disc of a food processor or slice strawberries by hand. Stir in sugar. Taste and correct sweetness. Add Grand Marnier and orange peel. Stir to combine. Cover and chill thoroughly before serving. Makes 6 servings.

Fruit Brûlée

This delicious recipe can be made with seedless green grapes, peaches, strawberries, blueberries or raspberries.

3 cups fruit
1 cup sour cream
1 tsp. vanilla
1 cup firmly packed brown sugar

Place fruit in a 9-inch glass pie pan or other shallow ovenproof dish. In a small bowl, combine sour cream and vanilla. Pour over fruit. Sprinkle evenly with brown sugar. Broil until sugar caramelizes. Watch carefully because the sugar needs to melt but not burn. Cover and refrigerate several hours before serving. Serves 4 to 6.

Hot Spiced Fruit

This easily assembled dish is particularly nice to serve in the fall and winter months. It can be served as a side dish or as a dessert. It goes nicely with ham.

3 oranges
3 lemons
1/2 cup firmly packed brown sugar
2 cans (1 lb. each) apricot halves,
    drained
2 cans (1 lb. each) pineapple chunks,
    drained

2 cans (1 lb. each) sliced peaches,
    drained
1 tsp. freshly grated nutmeg
1 cup sour cream (for topping)

Grate rind of one orange and one lemon. Set these aside for another use. Combine grated rind with brown sugar. Cut remaining 2 oranges and 2 lemons into paper thin slices, including their skins. Layer canned fruits and citrus slices alternately with brown-sugar mixture in a shallow ovenproof serving dish. Top with grated nutmeg. Bake at 325°F. for 20 minutes, or until hot and bubbly. Serve with a dollop of sour cream. Serves 8 to 10.

Rum-Baked Fruit

Serve this dessert just barely warm. The vivid colors are particularly appealing.

1 can (16 ozs.) pear halves
1 can (16 ozs.) peach halves
1 can (16 ozs.) apricot halves
1 can (16 ozs.) pitted bing cherries
2 boxes (10 ozs. each) frozen
    strawberries, thawed

1 cup firmly packed brown sugar
1/2 cup rum
2 cups sour cream (for serving)

Drain canned fruits, reserving 1/2 cup of any juice. Layer fruits in a pretty ovenproof baking dish. Top with thawed berries. Sprinkle brown sugar evenly over top. Drizzle with reserved fruit juice and rum. Bake at 350°F. for 20 minutes, or until heated through. Remove from oven and let cool a bit. Serve warm, topped with a dollop of sour cream. Serves 8.

Orange Delight

So simple to put together and so refreshing. Serve with a small cookie as a simple dessert for a summer brunch.

1/2 gallon vanilla ice cream, softened
1 can (12 ozs.) frozen orange juice concentrate, thawed
1/2 cup Grand Marnier liqueur

Combine all ingredients in a large mixing bowl, stirring until smooth. Place in a covered container and refreeze. Makes 8 to 12 servings.

Hint: Sugar-coated mint leaves make a lovely garnish for this dessert. To prepare: remove stems and wash mint leaves. Dip in beaten egg white and then in granulated sugar. Set on a wire rack to dry.

Melon With Port

This is an easy and novel way to serve honeydew melon. To test a melon for ripeness, check its fragrance—it should smell sweet. The stem end should be slightly sunken and calloused.

1 honeydew melon
1 cup port wine
sprig of mint or orange slice for garnish

Cut a plug in the melon, 1 inch in diameter. Pour wine into hole and reinsert plug. Refrigerate overnight. Before serving, drain wine. Cut melon into slices and remove seeds. Garnish with mint or an orange slice, if desired. Serves 4 to 8.

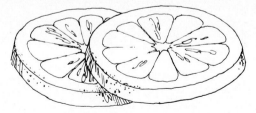

Cold Strawberry Soup

A refreshing "starter" during the summer months. Serve in pretty cups and garnish with whipped cream if desired.

2 quarts fresh or frozen strawberries
1 cup sugar
2 cups water
1/4 cup fresh lemon juice

grated rind of one orange
grated rind of one lemon
about 2 cups Rhine wine, chilled
whipped cream for garnish (optional)

Wash and hull berries. Purée in blender or use steel knife of food processor. Set aside. Combine sugar and water in medium-sized saucepan. Boil for 10 minutes to make sugar syrup. Cool. Add strawberry purée to syrup. Add lemon juice and grated citrus rind. Stir well. Cover and chill several hours or overnight. Before serving, stir in chilled wine to desired consistency. Garnish, if desired, with whipped cream. Serves 8 to 10.

Iced Cantaloupe Soup

For a change of pace try this refreshing soup. Mint leaves or a nasturtium blossom make an attractive garnish.

1 large, ripe cantaloupe
1/2 cup dry sherry
2 tbs. honey
1 tbs. fresh lime juice

Peel, seed and cube cantaloupe. Purée in food processor or blender. Add sherry, honey and lime juice. Taste to correct seasoning. Cover and chill overnight. Stir thoroughly before serving. Serves 4 to 6, depending upon size of the melon.

Nana's Fruit Soup

When I was a little girl, my Scandinavian grandmother "Nana" always made a batch of this fruit soup and left it early in the morning on our front porch for my birthday breakfast. Needless to say, the recipe is near and dear to me. You can serve this soup hot or cold. It should be very thick. You can add other canned or dried fruits, such as peaches, as your taste buds dictate.

1/2 cup pearl tapioca
3 cups water
1/2 cup raisins
1/2 cup pitted prunes
1 apple, peeled and thinly sliced

1 cup dried apricots
juice of one lemon
3 thin slices lemon
1 stick cinnamon
about 1/2 cup sugar (to taste)

Soak tapioca in water until soft and transparent, usually overnight. Combine with remaining ingredients in a large saucepan and simmer until fruits are tender and soft. Taste and add more sugar if desired. Serve hot or cold. Serves 6 to 8. Refrigerate any remaining soup. Keeps well in refrigerator for up to 2 weeks.

Tangy Raspberry Soup

If you have leftovers of this soup, pour it into ice cube trays or small paper cups for a frozen snack for the kids.

1 1/2 tbs. unflavored gelatin
1/3 cup cold water
3/4 cup hot water
3 pkgs. (10 ozs. each) frozen raspberries, thawed
3 1/2 cups sour cream or yogurt

1 1/3 cups pineapple juice
1 1/3 cups half and half
1 1/3 cups dry sherry, (optional)
1/3 cup grenadine
2 tbs. fresh lemon juice

Soak gelatin in cold water for 5 minutes in a small saucepan. Add hot water and place over low heat, shaking pan until gelatin is completely dissolved. Remove from heat. Purée berries in food processor or blender. Strain raspberries to remove seeds. Combine with gelatin in a large glass bowl. Stir in remaining ingredients until mixture is smooth. Cover and refrigerate overnight. Serves 12.

Quick Fruit Ideas

- For a creative "bowl" to hold a fruit compote: use a pineapple sliced lengthwise or crosswise and hollowed; or any kind of melon (watermelon, cantaloupe, honeydew or casaba) cut in half and hollowed.
- Loosen the skin from a fully ripe yet firm peach by submerging it in boiling water for several minutes (not too long or the peach will cook). Remove skin and discard. Carefully slice peach in half. Remove seed. Place each half in a tall goblet. Cover with ice-cold champagne.
- Make a raspberry sauce to serve over fresh, sliced strawberries OR oranges by puréeing one 10-ounce package of frozen raspberries with 2 tablespoons of sugar, 1 tablespoon of Grand Marnier and 1 teaspoon of fresh lemon juice.
- For a real show-stopper, whip up some Fruit Flambèe. In a saucepan, melt 3 tablespoons of butter over low heat. Stir in 3 tablespoons of firmly packed brown sugar. Add to saucepan: 1 banana, sliced once lengthwise and once crosswise OR 4 slices of pineapple, drained. Simmer until warmed through, about 5 minutes. In a separate saucepan, heat 1/4 cup brandy, cognac OR rum. Place fruit and sauce in a pretty serving bowl. Pour liquor over fruit. Ignite and serve.

- Wrap one or two paper-thin slices of prosciutto around cantaloupe, casaba OR honeydew melon, peeled and sliced kiwi fruit OR pear slices.
- For delicious and unusual Baked Apples: wash and core whole apples. Stuff each core with a mixture of 1 tablespoon of softened butter, 2 tablespoons of firmly packed brown sugar and 1/8 to 1/4 teaspoon EACH of cinnamon and cloves . If desired, drizzle with about 1 tablespoon of honey before baking. Place apples in a shallow baking pan. Fill pan with water to a depth of 1/4 inch. Bake at 350°F for 30 minutes, or until tender when pierced with a fork. Some other creative fillings are: cooked, crumbled sausage, mincemeat or granola.
- For Hawaiian Peaches: fill a large perfect peach half with a teaspoon of firmly packed brown sugar, 1 tablespoon of crushed pineapple (or pineapple juice) and 1 teaspoon of firm butter. Dust with cinnamon OR nutmeg OR cloves. Bake at 350°F for 12 to 15 minutes, or until bubbly. Serve warm with a dollop of sour cream, if desired.
- Add a bit of romance to your next brunch by preparing Italian Pears. Fill well-drained, canned pear halves with a mixture of 2 tablespoons of butter, 1/8 teaspoon of almond extract and 1/4 cup of finely chopped almonds. Place pears in a baking pan. Drizzle with 1/3 cup cream sherry. Bake at 350°F for 30 minutes.

Egg Dishes And Main Dishes

Flavorful, versatile and nutritious, eggs are a star attraction for brunches. Hard cooked, fried, poached, scrambled, baked or made into an omelet, frittata or quiche, economical egg dishes can be relied upon to provide delicious and interesting main dishes for any occasion. Cheese and eggs have a great affinity for one another and the combinations possible are numerous. Most of the egg dishes offered in this chapter can be assembled partially or entirely in advance, making them ideal for brunch.

When I studied cooking at the Cordon Bleu in London I was amazed to find the British did not refrigerate eggs. They literally keep eggs for weeks and weeks at room temperature. When a fresh egg was called for in a recipe, it was called a "new laid" egg.

Eggs with Tomatoes, Bacon and Hollandaise, p. 58.

Basic Omelet

Once you have mastered the technique of omelet making, you'll rely on it again and again to make a variety of delicious combinations. Omelets take only a few minutes to make, so each one can be made to order. Have guests join you in the kitchen. They'll enjoy the fun.

For each omelet:
3 eggs
1 tbs. butter

Break eggs into a small mixing bowl. Beat with a whisk 30 to 40 strokes. Place omelet pan over medium-high heat. Melt butter until it sizzles. Quickly pour in eggs. Let omelet set a second. Lift cooked edge and let uncooked egg run underneath. Shake pan to keep omelet from sticking. When eggs are cooked but top is still moist and creamy, add about 1/4 cup of filling down the center or on one half of the omelet. Use a spatula to fold the sides or other half over the filling. Tilt out onto plate. Makes one omelet.

About Omelet Pans: A good omelet pan is the key to successful omelets. Use a pan with a flat bottom, sloping sides, the top approximately 9 inches in diameter. It should be used only for omelets and should not be washed or soaked, merely rinsed with hot water after use. If scouring is necessary, pour a little salt in and rub with a paper towel.

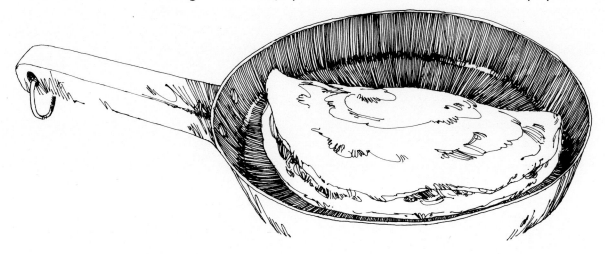

Ideas for Omelet Fillings

Cold Fillings:
- cavier and sour cream
- smoked salmon, sour cream and chopped green onions
- chutney and chopped toasted almonds
- canned, dried onion rings
- crab, cream cheese and alfalfa sprouts
- sour cream, avocado and Mexican salsa sauce
- chopped watercress and sour cream
- diced cooked chicken, avocado and sour cream
- green onions, avocado and cooked crumbled bacon
- ripe olives, green onions, tomatoes and sour cream

- sliced strawberries and sour cream
- cooked tiny shrimp, tomatoes, green onions and sour cream
- diced canned green chiles, tomatoes and grated Cheddar
- crumbled cooked bacon and avocado with alfalfa sprouts
- shredded cheeses: Swiss, Cheddar, Monterey Jack, Parmesan

Hot Fillings:

Cook any one of the following combinations in butter until heated through:

- sautéed chicken livers and mushrooms
- asparagus spears; garnish with shredded Cheddar
- julienned ham and chopped green onions
- diced artichoke hearts; garnish with Parmesan
- diced salami, sweet onion and green pepper
- lobster chunks, and a bit of dry sherry wine

- add any one of the following to basic cheese or cream sauce: mushrooms, shrimp, crab, chicken, turkey, salmon
- cooked crumbled sausage
- hot apple pie filling
- canned Chinese-style vegetables
- canned chili, diced raw onion and shredded Cheddar

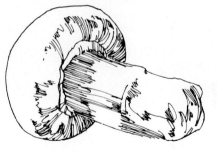

Poached Egg Instructions

What some folks don't realize is that eggs can be poached at your leisure, refrigerated for as long as 24 hours and used at your convenience. This makes them ideal for brunch and avoids last-minute cooking.

In a large, deep, buttered skillet, bring to a boil enough water to cover eggs. Add one tablespoon mild vinegar. Break each egg into a small saucer. Slide carefully into gently bubbling water. Quickly spoon hot water over each egg to film the yolk. Cook no more than 4 eggs at a time. Simmer the eggs gently for 3 to 4 minutes, or until egg holds its shape, the white is firm and the yolk is still soft. With a slotted spoon, gently lift each egg out of the water and place on a paper towel to drain. Trim any excess pieces of white (called "oddments" at the Cordon Bleu) from the egg to make a nice shape. Eggs may either be used immediately or covered with cold water and stored in a covered container in the refrigerator.

To reheat, cover the eggs with very hot water for 5 to 10 minutes, or until eggs are heated through.

Crabby Benedict

This is an easy and luxurious variation of Eggs Benedict. Serve it with an assortment of fresh fruits and cheeses, a crisp white wine and something nutty and gooey for dessert.

1 lb. crab meat
8 whole canned artichoke bottoms
4 whole English muffins, split, toasted and buttered
8 poached eggs (see page 56)
2 cups Hollandaise sauce, page 146

Drain artichokes and pat them dry. Remove and discard any cartilage from crab. Place a bed of crab on each muffin half. Top with an artichoke bottom. Place poached egg over all. Warm in oven at 200°-250°F. while preparing Hollandaise. When muffins are warmed through, top with sauce and serve. Serves 4 to 8.

Eggs with Tomatoes, Bacon and Hollandaise

For a change of pace from traditional Eggs Benedict try this idea. For variety, use a nippy Cheddar cheese sauce instead of Hollandaise.

4 whole English muffins
2 large, ripe, firm tomatoes
8 slices bacon, cooked crisp and crumbled (reserve drippings)
8 poached eggs
1 recipe Hollandaise, page 146
1/4 cup all-purpose flour
1/2 tsp. salt
1/2 tsp. pepper

Prepare poached eggs according to recipe on page 56. Split, toast and butter English muffins. Cut tomatoes into 8 slices, approximately 1/2 inch thick each. Dip in flour. Fry tomatoes in reserved bacon drippings until tender and golden, about 5 minutes. Sprinkle with salt and pepper. To assemble: Place a tomato slice on each muffin half, top with poached egg, nap with Hollandaise and sprinkle with crumbled bacon. Serves 4.

Swiss Cheese and Egg Casserole

This method of preparing an egg casserole is exceptionally creamy and rich.

2 cups soft bread cubes, crusts removed
1 3/4 cups half and half
8 eggs, slightly beaten
2 tbs. butter
1 tsp. seasoned salt
1/2 tsp. pepper

1 cup shredded Swiss cheese
8 slices bacon, cooked crisp and
    crumbled
1/2 cup fine dry bread crumbs (use crusts
    from bread)
2 tbs. butter, melted

In a small bowl, combine bread cubes with half and half. Let soak five minutes. Drain liquid from bread cubes. Add to eggs. Beat well. Melt 2 tablespoons of butter in a heavy skillet. Add egg mixture. Softly scramble eggs over medium heat. When eggs are still soft but almost cooked through, add soaked bread cubes to eggs. Stir to combine. Sprinkle with seasoned salt and pepper. Pour egg mixture into a lightly greased ovenproof casserole about 10 inches in diameter. Top with shredded cheese, crumbled bacon and dry bread crumbs. Drizzle with the melted butter. Bake at 400°F. for 10 to 15 minutes, or until heated through and cheese is melted. Cut in squares to serve. Makes 8 servings.

Fantastic Mushroom Eggs with Cheese and Cream Sauce

This rich dish has delighted my students for years. Experiment with it by using other types of cheeses. I usually have quite an assortment on hand. From time to time I shred them all in my Cuisinart and toss them into a plastic bag. Then whenever I need shredded cheese, I remove the bag from the freezer, let it set a moment or two, and PRESTO, I have a rich and varied assortment of shredded cheese.

For the mushrooms:
2 tbs. butter
1 lb. fresh mushrooms, thinly sliced

For the eggs:
1 dozen eggs
1/2 cup butter
salt, pepper—a dash each

Melt 2 tablespoons of butter in a large skillet over medium heat. Sauté mushrooms until soft. Sprinkle with salt and pepper. Set aside. Break eggs into a large bowl and whisk thoroughly. Add salt and pepper. Melt half of the 1/2 cup butter in a large skillet over very low heat. Pour eggs into skillet. Gently scramble eggs. When eggs have turned into very soft curds, stir in remaining butter and sprinkle with salt and pepper. Set aside. Make a cream sauce and shred the cheeses:

Sauce:
6 tbs. butter
6 tbs. all-purpose flour
1 pint half-and-half
salt, pepper—a dash each

Cheeses:
4 ozs. Parmesan cheese, grated
4 ozs. Swiss or Gruyére cheese, grated
4 ozs. Cheddar cheese, grated

Melt butter in a saucepan over medium-low heat. Stir in flour. Allow mixture to bubble for 30 seconds. Add salt and pepper. Stir in cream. Whisk over low heat until mixture thickens. Meanwhile, grate cheeses.

To Assemble:

Lightly butter the bottom of a large ovenproof casserole. Sprinkle with half of the Parmesan. Spread a thin layer of the cream sauce over cheese. Place half of the scrambled eggs on top. Add half of the remaining cream sauce to mushrooms, stir. Place mushroom mixture on top of the eggs. Sprinkle with half of the grated Swiss and Cheddar. Add rest of eggs. Top with remaining cream sauce. Sprinkle with remaining Swiss, Cheddar and Parmessan. Broil 6 inches from the heat until cheese is bubbly and eggs are heated through. Serves 6 to 8.

Cotswold Cheese Flan

This recipe is from the Cotswold region of England, where they make a nippy cheese, similar to Cheddar, which contains chives. This flan is good served hot, cold or at room temperature. You can use any plain pie crust, but the Shortcrust Pastry is exceptionally buttery and flaky.

Shortcrust Pastry:
1 1/2 cups all-purpose flour
1/2 cup butter, ice cold
1/4 cup shortening, ice cold
1 egg yolk
1/4 cup ice water

Filling:
1 large onion, peeled
1 tbs. butter
3/4 cup shredded sharp Cheddar
3 tbs. chopped chives
1 whole egg PLUS 1 egg yolk
1/4 cup cream or milk
1 tsp. salt
1/2 tsp. pepper
6 ozs. LARGE fresh mushrooms

Preheat oven to 400°F. Use a pastry cutter or the steel knife of a food processor to combine flour, butter and shortening until mixture resembles coarse cornmeal. Add egg yolk and sprinkle with water. Combine to make a soft dough. Roll out dough on a lightly floured surface. Line a 9-inch pie or quiche pan with dough. Bake blind* in oven until crust is just set, about 15 minutes. Meanwhile, cut onion into 1/8-inch slices. Melt butter in a large skillet over medium-low heat. Sauté onion until golden. Combine shredded cheese, chives, eggs and milk in a mixing bowl. Season with salt and pepper. Cut stems off mushrooms (and save them for another use). Place whole mushroom caps, stem side up, in the prepared crust.

Place sautéed onions over mushrooms. Pour cheese mixture over all. Return to oven for 15 to 20 minutes, or until mixture is set and brown. Let cool 10 minutes before cutting. Serves 6 to 8.

*To bake blind: Prick pastry shell with a fork. Line shell with foil, waxed paper or parchment paper, fill with dry beans, rice or metal pie weights to the depth of 1/2 inch. Bake as directed. Baking blind helps pastry to keep its shape.

Simply Elegant Quiche

This recipe is an adaptation of one from John McGarry, a White House chef during the Kennedy, Johnson and Nixon administrations. A delightful man with charm and good humor, he says this quiche was a favorite of Jackie Onassis and Henry Kissinger.

1/2 cup finely minced shallots
1/2 cup dry white wine
6 eggs
2 cups heavy cream
1 tsp. salt
1/4 tsp. white pepper

1/4 tsp. freshly grated nutmeg
6 ozs. shredded imported Gruyere
   cheese
1 prebaked 10-inch pie shell with
   a high rim

Place shallots and white wine in a small saucepan. Bring to a boil over low heat and simmer for 2 minutes. Remove and set aside to cool. Beat eggs and cream together very gently. Fold in shallot mixture and spices. Sprinkle cheese over bottom of prepared crust. Pour in custard mixture. Bake at 360°F. for 35 to 45 minutes, or until custard is set. Cover edges of pie crust with foil if crust gets too dark. Let quiche set for 10 minutes prior to serving. Serves 6 to 8.

Simply Elegant Quiche,

Quiche A La Provençale

If you have vegetarian friends, this quiche makes a delightful main dish. Add a simple green salad, fruit and cheese to complete your menu.

1 egg, lightly beaten
1 tbs. water
One 10-inch unbaked pie shell
1 pkg. (6 ozs.) long-grain and
    wild rice mix
2 tbs. olive oil
2 cloves garlic, minced

1 can (14 ozs.) Italian plum tomatoes
    (2 cups)
1 pkg. (8 ozs.) cream cheese
1 tsp. salt
1/4 tsp. pepper
4 eggs, lightly beaten

Beat 1 egg with 1 tablespoon of water to make a glaze. Brush about 1 tablespoon over pie shell and bake at 375°F. for 10 minutes. Remove from oven and set aside while making filling. Cook rice mix according to package directions. Heat olive oil in a small skillet over medium-low heat. Sauté garlic until limp. Combine hot cooked rice, garlic mixture, tomatoes, cream cheese, salt and pepper. Stir until cream cheese is melted. Stir a small amount of this hot mixture into 4 beaten eggs. Return egg mixture to the rice mixture and blend well. Pour into prepared crust and bake at 375°F. for 30 minutes, or until set. Let stand for 10 to 15 minutes before cutting and serving. Serves 6.

Hint: At the Cordon Bleu in London they mince garlic by flattening it with the side of a knife along with a generous teaspoon of salt. Continue to press and chop the garlic and salt mixture together until garlic is very finely crushed. This method works well in this recipe. If you use this method, however, don't forget to reduce the amount of salt in the recipe by 1 teaspoon.

Klara's Crab Quiche

This recipe is from a good friend who is an extraordinarily good cook. The herbed crust adds a nice touch.

Crust:
1 cup all-purpose flour
1/2 tsp. onion salt
1/8 tsp. basil
2 tbs. ice cold butter
2 tbs. ice cold shortening
3 tbs. ice water
Filling:
8 ozs. crabmeat, fresh or canned
6 slices bacon, cooked crisp and
     crumbled

1 tbs. cornstarch
2 cups half and half
4 eggs
1/2 tsp. salt
1/4 tsp. nutmeg
dash of red pepper
2 cups shredded Swiss cheese
Topping:
2 tbs. melted butter
2 tbs. grated Parmesan

Prepare crust. Combine flour, onion salt and basil in mixing bowl. Cut butter and shortening into flour mixture until it resembles coarse cornmeal. Sprinkle with ice water.

Stir with fork until mixture forms a ball. Knead a few times. Chill in plastic wrap or wax paper while making filling.

Remove any cartilage from crabmeat. Mix together crabmeat, bacon and cornstarch. Set aside. In another bowl, beat together half-and-half, eggs, salt, nutmeg and red pepper. Set aside while you roll out pastry. Remove pastry from refrigerator. On a well-floured board, roll dough to fit a 9 or 10-inch quiche pan. Gently place pastry in quiche pan. Prick with fork. Bake at 425°F. for about 7 minutes, or until crust is just beginning to turn golden brown. Place crabmeat, bacon and cornstarch in partially baked pastry shell. Sprinkle with Swiss cheese. Pour half and half mixture over all. Drizzle with Topping ingredients. Bake at 375°F. for about 40 minutes, or until custard is set. Let stand 10 minutes before cutting. Serves 6 to 8.

Note: Sometimes I use this recipe as an appetizer. To do this, line a 9 x 13-inch pan with the pastry. Bake it partially as directed above. Add filling ingredients in order. Bake at 375°F. for 20 to 30 minutes. Cut into squares and serve. Makes about 15 appetizer servings.

Zucchini Quiche with Cheese Crust

This savory crust can also be used for a seafood, broccoli or spinach quiche. Avoid using Cheddar cheese in the filling, as it would be too similar to the crust.

Cheese Crust:
1 cup all-purpose flour
1/2 cup butter, ice cold, cut into cubes
2 ozs. Velveeta brand cheese, cut into
    cubes
1 tbs. ice water
dash Tabasco sauce

Filling:
1/4 cup butter
1/2 cup sliced onion

4 cups unpeeled and thinly sliced zucchini
1 small clove garlic, minced
1/2 cup chopped parsley
2 eggs
1 cup half and half
1 cup shredded Mozzarella cheese
1/2 tsp. EACH salt and pepper
1/4 tsp. EACH oregano and basil

Make Crust. Combine all crust ingredients in a food processor or a mixing bowl. Process or beat until a ball of dough forms. Wrap dough in plastic wrap and chill for 10 minutes.

Prepare Filling. Melt butter in a large skillet over medium heat. Sauté onion, zucchini and garlic in butter for 10 minutes, stirring occasionally. Stir in parsley and set aside. Preheat oven to 375°F. Remove crust dough from refrigerator. Roll out on a heavily floured surface. Line a 10-inch pie or quiche pan with dough. Prick entire surface with fork. Beat together eggs and half-and-half. Use 1 tablespoon of egg mixture to glaze crust before baking. Place crust in oven and bake for 10 minutes. Mix together cheese and remaining egg mixture. Add salt, pepper, oregano and basil to vegetable mixture. Toss gently. Pour egg and cheese mixture into vegetable mixture. Stir to combine. Pour into prepared crust and continue baking for 15 to 20 minutes, or until center is set. Cover edges with foil if they begin to brown too quickly. Let quiche stand at room temperature for 10 minutes prior to serving. Serves 6 to 8.

Easy Chicken Divan

This recipe has been one of my favorites for years. A fresh fruit salad and hot muffins sit just right with this.

2 pkgs. (10 ozs. each) frozen chopped broccoli
3 whole chicken breasts, cooked
1 can (10 ozs.) condensed cream of chicken soup, undiluted
1 cup mayonnaise
2 tsp. fresh lemon juice
4 ozs. shredded sharp Cheddar
1 cup crushed potato chips

Cook broccoli according to package directions. Drain and place in the bottom of an 11 x 7-inch ovenproof casserole. Cut chicken into large slivers and place on top of broccoli. In a small bowl combine soup, mayonnaise and lemon juice. Pour over chicken and broccoli. Top with shredded cheese and sprinkle with potato chips. Bake at 350°F. for 35 to 40 minutes, or until hot and bubbly. Serves 6.

Crab Casserole Florentine

2 tbs. butter
2 pkgs. (10 ozs. each) frozen chopped
    spinach, thawed and drained
1 can (10 ozs.) cream of mushroom
    soup, undiluted
1 can (10 ozs.) prepared white sauce
1 1/4 cups shredded Swiss cheese

1 tbs. fresh lemon juice
2 cans (7 1/2 ozs. each) crabmeat,
    drained
1 can (6 ozs.) water chestnuts, drained
    and sliced
3 tbs. grated Parmesan cheese

Melt butter in large skillet over medium heat. Add spinach and cook until all liquid has evaporated. Stir in mushroom soup. Remove from heat and set aside. Combine white sauce, cheese and lemon juice in a saucepan. Cook over medium heat, stirring until cheese melts. Remove cartilage from crabmeat. Add to sauce along with water chestnuts. In an ovenproof casserole, about 10 inches in diameter, make a layer of the spinach and mushroom soup using one half the mixture. Top with half of the crab mixture. Repeat layers. Sprinkle top with Parmesan. Bake at 300°F. for 1 hour. Serves 6 to 8. May be prepared ahead up to 2 days in advance and refrigerated; increase baking time 10 minutes.

Shrimp and Cheese Strata

Sour cream adds special tang to this Strata. Although the texture is similar to soufflés, Stratas are much less temperamental.

6 slices firm white bread, crusts removed
4 tbs. melted butter
1 cup grated Swiss cheese
2 green onions, chopped
2 tbs. chopped parsley
1/2 lb. tiny cooked shrimp

3 eggs
1/2 tsp. salt
1/2 tsp. Dijon mustard
1 1/2 cups milk
1/2 cup sour cream

Cut each slice of bread in half on the diagonal. Dip in melted butter. Arrange half of the slices in an unbuttered 8-inch baking dish. Sprinkle with half of the cheese, onions, parsley and shrimp. Add remaining bread and repeat process. Beat eggs, salt, mustard, milk and sour cream together. Pour over casserole. Cover and chill overnight. Bake at 350°F. for 30 to 40 minutes, or until puffed and golden. Cut into squares and serve. Serves 6 to 8.

Cheese Strata

Stratas have endless variations and are perfect for making the night before a brunch. Once on summer vacation I filled in unexpectedly for a chef and made a Strata for breakfast that used 10 dozen eggs and 15 pounds each of sausage and cheese!

9 slices bread, cubed
1 1/2 tbs. instant minced onion
1 lb. sharp Cheddar cheese, grated
3 eggs
3 cups milk
1 tsp. EACH dry mustard and
    Worcestershire sauce
1/2 tsp. EACH salt and pepper

Optional: add one of the following:
1/2 lb. bacon, cooked crisp and
    crumbled
1/2 lb. sausage, cooked and drained
1 cup cubed cooked ham, turkey or
    chicken
1 cup shrimp or crab
1 cup sautèed mushrooms

Butter a 2-quart baking dish. Layer bread, onion, cheese and the optional ingredients in the casserole. Beat eggs, milk and seasonings together. Pour over bread mixture. Cover and let stand overnight in refrigerator. Bake at 325°F. for 1 hour, or until puffed and center is set. Serves 8.

Cheese and Chilies Casserole

Nice accompaniments for this casserole are Brandied Fresh Fruit, Sour Cream Coffee Cake and Mexican Coffee.

2 cans (4 ozs. each) diced green chilies
1 lb. Monterey Jack cheese, shredded
1 lb. Cheddar cheese, shredded
4 eggs, separated (at room
    temperature)

1 small can (5.3 ozs.) evaporated milk
1 tbs. all-purpose flour
1/2 tsp. EACH salt and pepper
2 fresh tomatoes, sliced

Toss together chilies and cheese. Place in a well-buttered shallow 2-quart ovenproof casserole. Beat egg whites until stiff peaks form. Combine yolks, evaporated milk, flour, salt and pepper in a medium sized bowl. Beat well. Fold in egg whites. Pour egg mixture over cheese and chilies. Bake at 325°F. for 30 minutes. Remove from oven and arrange tomato slices attractively over the top. Continue baking for 30 minutes, or until knife inserted into center comes out clean. Serves 8.

Easy Baked Eggs

For variety, try substituting crumbled, cooked bacon for the ham and add one cup sautéed mushrooms to the mixture. Other varieties of cheese may be used as well; Swiss, Monterey Jack, or a combination of cheeses would be tasty.

2 tbs. butter
6 green onions, thinly sliced
12 eggs, beaten
1 1/3 cups milk

3/4 tsp. seasoned salt
1 1/2 cups diced ham
3 cups shredded Cheddar cheese

Melt butter in a skillet over medium-low heat. Sauté onions in butter until soft. In a large mixing bowl, beat eggs. Add milk, salt, ham and all but 1/2 cup of the cheese. Pour egg mixture into a greased oven proof 2-quart casserole. Bake uncovered at 350°F. for 30 minutes, or until mixture is set. Remove from oven and sprinkle with remaining cheese. Continue to bake until cheese melts. Serves 8.

Fresh Pan-Fried Trout

A brunch any fisherman will adore! Serve with red-skinned home fries, sunnyside-up eggs, sliced ripe tomatoes, Crumbly Walnut Coffee Cake, and plenty of hot coffee.

4 fresh trout (8 to 10 ozs. each)
2 tsp. salt
1/4 tsp. freshly ground black pepper
1/2 cup yellow cornmeal
1/2 cup all-purpose flour

3 tbs. butter
6 tbs. vegetable oil
8 slices crisp bacon (optional)
fresh parsley (optional)
lemon wedges (optional)

Wash trout briefly under cold running water. Pat dry with paper towels. Sprinkle cavities and skins of fish with salt and pepper. Mix cornmeal and flour together on a large plate. Dip trout in mixture, shaking off excess. Melt butter with oil in a heavy 12-inch skillet over medium heat. Fry trout 4 to 5 minutes on each side, until golden brown, crisp and firm to the touch. Arrange trout on heated platter and garnish with bacon, parsley and lemon, if desired. Serve immediately. Serves 4.

Seafood Frittata

Frittatas are open-faced Italian omelets. They are cooked slowly over very low heat until firm and set, but not dry or stiff. Make them round and cook them on both sides. Cheese, vegetables, herbs, seafood and various meats are among the fillings used for Frittatas.

6 eggs
1/4 tsp. EACH salt and pepper
3 tbs. butter
1/4 cup coarsely chopped onion
1/2 cup sliced mushrooms

1/4 lb. tiny bay scallops
1/4 lb. fresh cooked crab
1/4 lb. fresh cooked shrimp
1 cup grated Parmesan OR Swiss cheese
3 tbs. butter

Beat eggs in a bowl. Add salt and pepper. Set aside. Melt butter in a heavy-bottomed skillet over medium heat. Sauté onion and mushrooms in butter until limp. Add scallops and cook for just a few minutes, until opaque. Stir crab and shrimp into skillet. Remove pan from heat. Stir about three quarters of the cheese into the eggs. Add cooked seafood mixture to egg and cheese mixture and blend thoroughly. Wipe skillet out with a paper towel. Add remaining 3 tablespoons of butter to skillet. Place over medium heat. When

butter begins to foam, add egg and seafood mixture. Turn heat down to low. Cook eggs without stirring, until set and thickened, about 10 minutes. Preheat broiler.

When only the top is still moist, sprinkle with remaining cheese and place skillet under broiler until top is lightly golden brown. Loosen Frittata with a spatula and slide it onto a warm plate. Cut into wedges and serve. Serves 4 to 6.

Fresh Vegetable Frittata

For variety, add about 3/4 cup of cooked crumbled sausage or ground beef to this mixture. Fill pineapple shells or melon halves with seasonal fresh fruits and choose one of the coffee cakes to round out your brunch.

6 eggs
1/2 tsp. EACH salt and pepper
3 tbs. butter
3 small zucchini, sliced
1 large onion, sliced
1 clove garlic, minced
1 cup fresh mushrooms, sliced

2 cups fresh spinach, washed and
    cut into 1-inch strips
1 tbs. chopped parsley
1 tsp. Italian herb seasoning
1 cup grated Parmesan OR Swiss cheese
3 tbs. butter

Beat eggs in bowl. Add salt and pepper. Set aside. Melt 3 tablespoons butter in a heavy-bottomed skillet over medium heat. Sauté zucchini, onion, garlic and mushrooms until limp. Add spinach and toss until wilted. Sprinkle with parsley and Italian seasoning. Remove pan from heat. Stir about three quarters of the cheese into the eggs. Add cooked vegetable mixture to egg and cheese mixture and blend thoroughly. Wipe skillet out with

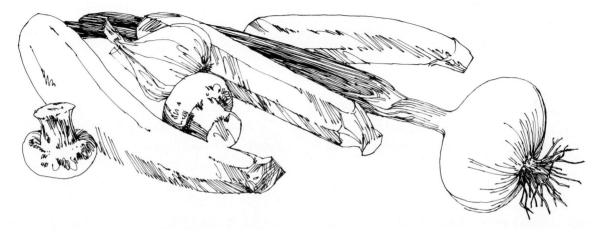

a paper towel. Add remaining 3 tablespoons of butter to skillet. Place over medium heat. When butter begins to foam, add egg and vegetable mixture and turn heat down to low. Cook eggs without stirring until set and thickened, about 10 minutes. Preheat broiler. When only the top is still moist, sprinkle with remaining cheese and place skillet under broiler until top is light golden brown. Loosen Frittata with a spatula and slide it onto warm plate. Cut into wedges and serve. Serves 4 to 6.

Savory Chicken Tart

Maureen Reynolds, author of Nitty Gritty's Convection Oven Cookbook, uses ham in a similar recipe in her book. You can also serve it as an appetizer.

Filling:
2 tbs. butter
1 cup finely diced cooked chicken
2 tbs. chopped chives OR green onions
2 egg yolks
1/4 cup cream
1/4 tsp. Worcestershire sauce
dash of Tabasco sauce

1/4 tsp. EACH salt and pepper
1/2 cup grated Swiss OR Parmesan
 cheese

Crust:
1 pkg. Pepperidge Farm frozen patty
 shells, thawed
1 egg, beaten
2 tbs. grated Parmesan

Make filling. Melt butter in skillet over medium heat. Stir in chicken and chives. Sauté for 2 minutes. In a small bowl beat together egg yolks, cream, Worcestershire, Tabasco, salt, pepper. Stir quickly into chicken mixture. Cook, stirring constantly, until mixture thickens. Remove from heat to cool. Stir in 1/2 cup cheese until melted. Set aside. Place 3 of the patty shells on a lightly floured surface. Roll out into a circle measuring 9 inches. Place on

84

a lightly buttered baking sheet. Brush edges of circle with beaten egg. Place chicken filling in center, mounding slightly. Roll out remaining 3 patty shells in the same manner. Place on top of filling. Press edges together with the tines of a fork. Brush with remaining beaten egg. Pierce with a fork. Sprinkle with Parmesan. Bake at 400°F. for 25 to 30 minutes, or until puffed and brown. Cut in wedges and serve piping hot. Serves 6.

Side Dishes

For a change of pace, try Italian sausages instead of hash browns, ham or bacon. They go with almost any quiche or egg dish. To prepare them, prick each sausage 4 or 5 times with a fork. Place in a skillet and cover with water. Heat to gentle simmer. Poach for 20 minutes. Drain and cool. Refrigerate for up to 2 days prior to serving. When ready to serve, lightly butter a skillet. Cook sausages on medium heat until golden brown and piping hot. Cut into diagonal slices. Serve immediately on a warmed platter.

Broiled Tomatoes, p. 95
Sausage and Mushroom Strudel, p. 90

Sausage Ring

This very simple idea glorifies store bought sausage. Fill the center with scrambled eggs, creamed mushrooms, cooked vegetables or whatever suits your menu. Garnish your Sausage Ring with lots of fresh parsley sprigs and you have a feast for the eyes as well as the palate.

2 pkgs. (16 ozs. each) ground pork sausage
parsley sprigs

Press sausage firmly into a 9-inch ring mold. Bake at 350°F. for 45 minutes to 1 hour, or until pork is thoroughly cooked. Drain fat. Unmold sausage onto a heated serving plate. Fill center if desired. Garnish with parsley sprigs. Serves 6 to 8.

Sausages in a Pastry Shell

These fancy sausages make a tasty treat for a picnic or boating brunch. Serve them with an assortment of mustards.

1 pkg. (10 ozs.) frozen patty shells
12 pork sausage links, cooked (see page 86)

Thaw patty shells. Roll out on a lightly floured board into a 3 1/2 x 8-inch rectangle. Cut each rectangle in half to make two pieces, each 4 inches long. Split each cooked sausage in half lengthwise. Place on one side of dough, fold over other half. Moisten edges of pastry with water. Using a fork, press ends of pastry together to seal. Leave ends of sausage exposed. Place on ungreased baking sheet. Prick tops of pastry with fork. Bake at 400°F. for 25 minutes, or until golden brown. Serve warm or at room temperature. May be frozen. To reheat, bake frozen pastries at 400°F. for 8 minutes, or until heated through. Makes 12.

Sausage and Mushroom Strudel

Buttery, flaky pastry wraps around a creamy sausage and mushroom filling for an unusual and tasty treat. Purchase phyllo at your local delicatessen or in the gourmet section of your grocery store.

1 lb. bulk sausage
6 tbs. butter
2 tbs. oil
1 lb. fresh mushrooms, finely chopped
1/2 cup minced green onions
1 tsp. salt
1 tsp. pepper
1 pkg. (8 ozs.) cream cheese
12 sheets phyllo pastry
1 cup melted butter
1 cup fine dry bread crumbs.

Sauté sausage in a heavy skillet over medium heat until no pink remains. Drain thoroughly and set aside. In another skillet, melt butter with oil over medium heat. Add mushrooms and green onions and cook, stirring until liquid has evaporated. Stir in salt and pepper. Add cooked sausage and cream cheese, blending thoroughly. Lightly dampen a tea towel. Lay a sheet of phyllo on the towel. Brush with melted butter and sprinkle lightly with bread crumbs. Repeat four times, ending with sixth sheet of phyllo. Place half of the filling on the narrow edge of the phyllo, leaving a two-inch border on each side. Fold in sides and roll up pastry. Place roll on a buttered baking sheet. Brush with additional melted butter. Repeat procedure using remaining phyllo and sausage filling. Bake at 400°F. for 20 minutes or until golden. Serves 6 to 8.

Pineapple Casserole

A unique side dish that goes well with ham.

1/2 cup sugar
3 tbs. all-purpose flour
3 eggs
1 can (#2 size) unsweetened crushed pineapple
4 slices white bread, cut into 1/2-inch cubes
1/2 cup melted butter

In a mixing bowl combine sugar, flour and eggs. Stir in pineapple along with its juice. Pour into a buttered ovenproof casserole, about 9 inches square. Top with the cubed bread and drizzle with melted butter. Bake at 350°F. for 1 hour. Serves 6 to 8.

Corn Fritters

These crispy fritters add just the right touch to a breakfast of scrambled eggs, sausages and baked apples. Serve them with lots of heated maple syrup.

2 eggs, separated (at room temperature)
1 cup all-purpose flour
2 tsp. baking powder
1 can (15 ozs.) creamed corn
1/4 cup sugar
powdered sugar

Beat egg whites until stiff using an electric mixer. Place egg yolks in a separate bowl, beat slightly. Sift flour and baking powder into yolks and stir. Add creamed corn and sugar to egg yolk mixture, combining well. Fold in egg whites. Pour vegetable oil into a skillet to a depth of 1/2 inch. Heat oil to 375°F. Drop fritters by spoonfuls into hot oil. Don't crowd skillet. Cook until golden, turning once. Drain on paper towels. Sprinkle with powdered sugar. Keep warm in 200°F. oven while preparing the rest. Makes about 30 fritters.

Spinach "Soufflé"

Not a true "soufflé" this is assembled in just seconds with the aid of a food processor or blender. For variety, use broccoli instead of spinach. Top each serving with Rich Cheese Sauce, page 148, if desired.

1 pkg. (10 ozs.) frozen chopped spinach, thawed
1/2 cup cream
1 pkg. (8 ozs.) cream cheese, cubed
5 eggs

1/2 cup plus 1 tbs. grated Parmesan cheese
1/2 tsp. EACH salt and white pepper
pinch of nutmeg

Remove all excess moisture from spinach by placing it in a strainer and pressing with the back of a spoon. Place all ingredients, except 1 tablespoon cheese, in a blender or food processor. Blend or process until mixture is thoroughly combined. Butter a 1 1/2-quart soufflé dish. Sprinkle with reserved grated Parmesan. Pour mixture into prepared dish and bake at 375°F. for 50 minutes, or until puffed and golden. Serves 4 as a main dish and 6 as a side dish.

Broiled Tomatoes

These tasty tomatoes are a beautiful contrast to egg dishes. Remember not to overcook the tomatoes, as they continue to cook after being removed from the heat and lose their shape and color.

6 fresh tomatoes, unpeeled
1/2 cup fine dry bread crumbs
1/4 cup grated Parmesan cheese
1 tbs. minced chives OR green onions

1/4 cup minced parsley
1/4 cup melted butter
1/2 tsp. salt
1/2 tsp. pepper

Cut tomatoes in half crosswise or horizontally. Hold tomatoes upside down and press gently to remove seeds. Discard seeds. Place tomato halves in a lightly buttered baking dish. In a mixing bowl, combine remaining ingredients. Mix well. Divide mixture evenly on top of the prepared tomatoes. Broil 5 to 6 minutes or until piping hot and lightly browned. Serve's 6 to 12.

Mushroom Strata

This makes a nice side dish but can also be served as a main course. A fresh fruit compote and sausage links complete the menu.

1/4 cup butter
1 1/4 lb. fresh mushrooms, sliced
1/2 cup chopped onion
1/2 cup chopped celery
1/2 cup chopped green pepper
1/2 tsp. EACH salt and pepper
1/2 cup mayonnaise
6 slices bread, crusts removed
2 tbs. soft butter
2 eggs, beaten
1 1/2 cups milk
1 cup shredded Cheddar cheese

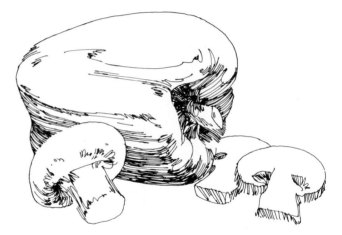

Melt butter in a large skillet over medium heat. Sauté mushrooms, onion, celery and green pepper until soft. Sprinkle with salt and pepper. Remove from heat and let cool. Stir in mayonnaise. Spread bread with soft butter. Cut bread into 1/2-inch cubes. Place half of the bread cubes in a lightly buttered 13 x 9 x 2-inch casserole. Pour sautéed vegetable mixture over top. Add remaining bread cubes. Beat eggs with milk and pour over casserole. Cover and refrigerate overnight. Bake casserole at 325°F. for 45 minutes. Remove from oven and sprinkle with cheese. Return to oven and continue baking for 15 minutes longer. Cut into squares and serve. Serves 8.

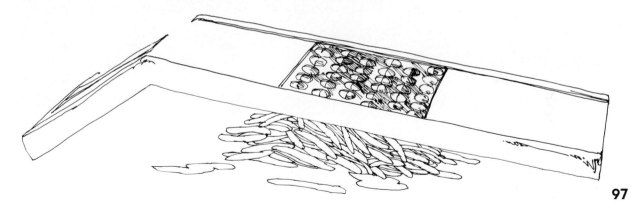

Quick Breads

What's more delightful than a piping hot muffin slathered with butter? (Muffins used to be sold hot, to warm the fingers; hence "little muffs.") Popovers are high, crusty shells with hollow insides, perfect for filling with creamed foods or just butter and jam. Scones are very much like biscuits, but richer.

One of the most memorable experiences of my life occured when I was visiting my friend Norman in England. At his country estate in Surrey, my friends and I were served a real English tea—practically a meal. We sat on his wide stone terrace in the sunshine and gentle breeze while the servants provided us with flaky hot scones dripping with thick Devonshire cream and gooseberry preserves. Sheer heaven!

Scones, p. 100

Scones

Handle Scone dough as gently as possible because the scones will be tough if the dough is overworked. Serve them with stiffly whipped cream and assorted jams along with a cup of bracing tea for a real British touch.

1 3/4 cups all-purpose flour	1/4 cup butter
2 tsp. baking powder	2 eggs, beaten
1 tbs. sugar	1/3 cup cream or milk
1/2 tsp. salt	1 tbs. sugar

Sift flour, baking powder, sugar and salt into a medium-sized bowl. Cut butter into flour mixture using a pastry blender or two knives. Mixture should resemble small peas. In another bowl, beat eggs and reserve 2 tablespoons for glaze. Beat all but 2 tablespoons of eggs with cream. Add to dry ingredients. Combine, using swift strokes. Divide dough into two balls. Pat each half out on a lightly floured board into a circle 3/4 inch thick. Cut each piece into 6 pie-shaped wedges. Place on a lightly buttered baking sheet. Brush with reserved beaten egg and sprinkle with sugar. Bake at 450°F. for 15 minutes, or until light gold. Makes 12 scones.

Popovers

For good Popovers, use a very hot oven and don't overbeat the batter. For cheese Popovers add 1/4 cup grated sharp Cheddar or Parmesan to the batter and a pinch of cayenne.

1 cup all-purpose flour
1/2 tsp. salt
1 cup milk
2 eggs

Preheat oven to 425°F. Thoroughly grease 12 muffin cups or custard cups. Do not use paper liners. Combine all ingredients and beat until just smooth using a rotary beater or whisk. Pour into prepared cups, filling about three quarters full. Bake 40 to 45 minutes on the lower rack of oven. Makes 9 to 12 popovers.

Lorna's Apple Bread

Moist and easy, this bread keeps well in the refrigerator for up to two weeks. A food processor makes preparing it a snap. Use it to chop the apple after it has been peeled and seeded.

2 cups finely diced apple,
    peeled and seeded
1 cup sugar
1/4 cup salad oil
1 egg, beaten
1 cup all-purpose flour

1/4 tsp. salt
1 tsp. baking soda
1 tsp. cinnamon
1/2 cup coarsely chopped walnuts
1/2 cup raisins OR currants

Toss apples with sugar in a large mixing bowl. Let stand 30 minutes. Add oil and egg, blending well. Sift flour, salt, soda and cinnamon into apple mixture. Stir thoroughly. Mix in nuts and raisins. Pour batter into a buttered and floured 9 x 5 x 3-inch bread pan. Bake at 350°F. for 50 to 60 minutes, or until bread tests done. Cool in pan for 10 minutes. Transfer to wire rack to complete cooling. To store, wrap in foil and refrigerate or freeze. Can be frozen up to 2 months. Makes 1 loaf.

Pumpkin Raisin Muffins

If you like, sprinkle the tops of these muffins with the Crunchy Nut Topping.

1 egg
1/2 cup milk
1/2 cup canned pumpkin
1/4 cup melted butter
1/2 cup sugar
1 1/2 cups all-purpose flour
2 tsp. baking powder

1/2 tsp. salt
1/2 tsp. EACH cinnamon and nutmeg
1/2 cup raisins
Nut Crunch Topping (optional):
1/3 cup firmly packed brown sugar
1/3 cup chopped walnuts
1/2 tsp. cinnamon

Combine egg, milk, pumpkin, butter and sugar in a medium-sized bowl. Stir until blended. Sift flour, baking powder, salt and 1/2 teaspoon each of cinnamon and nutmeg into pumpkin mixture. Stir until just moistened. Batter should be lumpy. Fold in raisins. Fill greased muffin cups about two thirds full. Combine Nut Crunch Topping ingredients in a small bowl. Sprinkle evenly over tops of muffins. Bake at 400°F. for 18 to 20 minutes. Serve hot. Makes 12 muffins.

Bran Muffins

The batter can be stored in the refrigerator for up to two weeks.

1 cup raisins OR chopped dates
1 tbs. baking soda
1 cup boiling water
1 cup sugar
1/2 cup butter
2 eggs
2 cups all-purpose flour

1/2 tsp. salt
1 cup All Bran cereal
2 cups raisin bran cereal
1 cup coarsely chopped walnuts
2 cups buttermilk
1 tsp. cinnamon
2 tbs. sugar

In a small bowl, combine raisins with baking soda and boiling water. Let cool. Cream sugar, butter and eggs together in a large mixing bowl until smooth. Add flour and salt. Stir until blended. Stir in cooled raisin mixture. Add remaining ingredients. Stir just until mixture is combined. Cover and refrigerate until ready to use. To bake muffins, generously butter muffin tins or line with paper muffin cups. Fill each tin two thirds full. Bake at 375°F. for 20 minutes, or until muffins test done. May be frozen for up to two months. Makes 4 1/2 dozen 3-inch muffins.

Three "C" Bread

Carrots, coconut and cherries give this quick bread its name.

3 eggs, beaten
1/2 cup vegetable oil
1/2 cup milk
1 cup sugar
2 1/2 cups all-purpose flour
1 tsp. EACH baking powder and
    baking soda

1 tsp. cinnamon
1/2 tsp. salt
2 cups shredded carrot
1 1/3 cups shredded coconut
1/2 cup chopped maraschino cherries
1/2 cup raisins
1/2 cup chopped pecans

In a large bowl, combine eggs, oil, milk and sugar. Beat well. Sift together flour, baking powder, baking soda, cinnamon and salt. Add to egg mixture. Stir until just moistened. Add carrot, coconut, cherries, raisins and nuts, blending thoroughly. Generously grease one 16-ounce tin can OR one 9 x 5 x 3-inch loaf pan. Pour batter into prepared pan. Bake at 350°F. for 45 to 50 minutes for cans, or 55 to 60 minutes for loaf pan. Let cool for 10 minutes before turning out to cool thoroughly. Wrap in foil and store in refrigerator or freezer. May be frozen for up to 2 months. Makes 1 can or 1 large loaf.

Walnut Streusel Muffins

This recipe was given to me by my friend, Carol. These muffins make any breakfast special. If you have any leftovers, tuck them in a lunchbox.

3/4 cup chopped walnuts
1 egg
1/2 cup honey
1/2 cup milk
1/4 cup melted shortening
1 3/4 cups all-purpose flour
2 1/2 tsp. baking powder
1 tsp. salt
1/2 cup chopped pitted dates

Cinnamon Streusel Topping:
1 tbs. firm butter
1 tbs. firmly packed brown sugar
1 tbs. all-purpose flour
1/2 tsp. cinnamon

Set aside 2 tablespoonfuls of walnuts for topping. Beat egg and honey together until well combined. Add milk and shortening. Stir well. Sift flour, baking powder and salt into egg mixture. Stir until just moist. Add dates and nuts. Stir briefly. Spoon into greased or paper-lined muffin tins, filling two thirds full. Prepare Topping. Cut butter into brown sugar.

106

Add flour, cinnamon and nuts. Mix until combined. Sprinkle about 1/2 teaspoon of mixture on top of unbaked muffins. Bake at 375°F. for 20 minutes. Let muffins cool for 5 minutes. Loosen edge with a small spatula or knife and turn out. Serve hot with butter and assorted jams. Makes 2 dozen 2 1/2-inch muffins. These muffins freeze well for up to 2 months.

Flavored Butters

Add a special touch to your brunch by serving a flavored butter with pancakes, waffles or quick breads.

Whip 1/2 cup of butter until fluffy and add one of the following combinations:
- 1/4 cup finely chopped toasted walnuts, 1/4 cup finely chopped golden raisins, 1 tablespoon orange juice, 1 tablespoon sugar and 1 teaspoon cinnamon
- 1/4 cup honey, 1 tablespoon orange juice, 2 teaspoons grated orange rind, 2 tablespoons sugar and 2 teaspoon cinnamon
- 1/2 cup marmalade or other jam, such as strawberry, peach, apricot or cherry
- 1 cup sifted powdered sugar, 1 teaspoon almond extract and 1/4 cup finely chopped toasted almonds
- 1/4 cup honey, 2 tablespoons orange juice and 1 small banana or peach, mashed
- 1/4 cup firmly packed sugar and 1/2 teaspoon EACH cinnamon and nutmeg

Special Marmalade

Turn store-bought marmalade into something special simply by adding a few extra ingredients.

Surprise friends with a calico-topped jar of your creation as a gift. Cut circles of calico 3 to 4 inches larger than the diameter of the jar (pinking shears leave a nice edge). Secure the calico with string or contrasting ribbon.

1 jar (8 ozs.) maraschino cherries
3 jars (16 ozs. each) orange marmalade
3 tbs. fresh lemon juice
1 cup coarsely chopped walnuts
1 cup golden raisins
paraffin (optional)

Drain and chop cherries. Combine with other ingredients in a large bowl. Spoon mixture into jars. Top each jar with a quarter inch of melted paraffin, if desired, or store jars in refrigerator. Makes about 8 cups.

Crêpes, French Toast and Pancakes

Some unusual and delicious recipes are included in this chapter. The versatile Crêpe is featured with both sweet and savory fillings. A custardy French Toast that can be prepared the night before your brunch is served with a variety of toppings. And of course, everyone's favorite: pancakes. Ordinary pancakes can easily be transformed into something special by adding any one of the following ingredients to your batter: blueberries, chocolate chips, sliced bananas, drained crushed pineapple or crumbled bacon.

I have been teaching cooking for years. Whenever I teach students how to make crêpes I bring along my "sacred crêpe pan." It's old, battered and simply indispensable for making crêpes. After years of study, I have what I believe to be the best method for making crêpes. It is detailed on the next page.

Shrimp and Asparagus Crepes Newburg, p. 116

Basic Crêpes

The versatility of crêpes is amazing. The variety of suitable fillings is virtually endless. They can be rolled, folded or stacked. They are easy, economical and elegant. And they can be made ahead and frozen until needed. What more can you ask?

The basic technique for making crêpes is easy once you have mastered the fundamentals. It is important that the pan be hot when the batter is poured into it. Tilt it immediately so that a thin layer of batter will cover the entire bottom.

3 eggs
1 1/3 cups milk
1 cup Wondra instant blending flour
1/4 tsp. salt
vegetable oil (not olive)

Combine all ingredients except oil using a blender, food processor or rotary beater. Batter should be smooth. Let it stand for 30 minutes-to allow the gluten in the flour to relax and the starch bubbles to burst, making a much lighter and more tender crêpe.

Place a crêpe pan or 8-inch skillet over moderately high heat until hot. Brush pan lightly with oil.

Pour 2 to 3 tablespoons batter into the center of the pan. Tilt pan and swirl batter to cover entire bottom and form a thin crêpe. Pour excess batter back into bowl. Cook crêpe 30 to 45 seconds, until light brown. Turn and cook briefly on the other side. Remove to plate. Trim off "handle" from crêpe that has resulted from pouring excess batter back into bowl. Repeat until all batter is used. Makes about sixteen 6-inch crêpes. They may be refrigerated for up to 2 days. Freeze for longer storage, separating them with waxed paper or foil. May be frozen for up to 3 months. They freeze best unfilled.

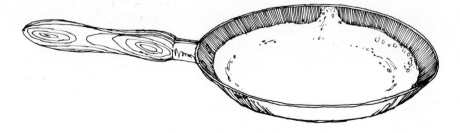

Beer Batter Crêpes

Beer adds a special flavor and makes crêpes lacy and delicate. Use this recipe with savory fillings.

3 eggs
1 cup milk
1 cup beer
1/2 tsp. salt
1 1/2 cups Wondra instant blending flour
3 tbs. melted butter or oil

Proceed, using same directions as for Basic Crêpes, page 112.

Sweet Crêpe Batter

An exceptionally delicate crêpe.

4 eggs
3/4 cup water
3/4 cup milk
2 tbs. sugar
1 1/2 cups all-purpose flour
3 tbs. brandy
1/2 tsp. salt
3 tbs. melted butter

Proceed, using same directions as for Basic Crêpes, page 112.

Shrimp and Asparagus Crêpes Newburg

1 1/4 cups asparagus, cut into
    1 to 1 1/2-inch lengths
2 tbs. butter
2 tbs. all-purpose flour
1 1/2 cups half-and-half
1 egg yolk

2 tbs. dry sherry or white wine
salt and white pepper
1 1/4 cups cooked, shelled and
    deveined baby shrimp
12 Basic Crêpes, page 112

Steam asparagus cuts until just tender, about 7 minutes. In another saucepan, melt butter over medium heat. Stir in flour. Let bubble 1 minute. Gradually add half-and-half. Beat with wire whisk until smooth and thickened, about 20 minutes. Remove mixture from heat. Mix a little of the hot cream sauce into the egg yolk. Beat well. While stirring, add egg yolk mixture to cream sauce. Stir well. Add sherry, salt and white pepper. Pour half of cream sauce into a bowl. Add shrimp and asparagus to remaining cream sauce in saucepan. Stir gently to combine, 3 to 4 strokes. Divide filling among crêpes. Roll. Place seam side down in a buttered, ovenproof serving dish. Bake at 350°F. for 10 to 15 minutes, until heated through. Pour reserved warm sauce over crêpes. Serve immediately. Serves 6.

Almond Crêpes Melba

1 recipe Sweet Crêpes, page 115
Almond Filling:
1/2 cup butter
1/2 cup sugar
1 egg
1/2 cup finely chopped almonds
2 tbs. Amaretto liqueur

Melba Sauce:
1 pkg. (10 ozs.) frozen raspberries,
    thawed
1/4 cup sugar
1/2 cup currant jelly
2 tbs. cornstarch
1 tbs. cold water

Prepare crêpes according to recipe. Combine all Almond Filling ingredients in a food processor or with electric beaters, process or beat until smooth. Spread a tablespoonful of the filling on each crêpe and roll up. Repeat with remaining filling and crêpes. Place crêpes in a buttered baking dish. May be refrigerated at this point for up to 1 day in advance. To bake, cover dish with foil. Bake at 425°F. for 15 minutes. Meanwhile prepare Melba Sauce. Strain raspberries to remove seeds, if desired. Heat raspberries, sugar and jelly in a saucepan until jelly melts. Mix together cornstarch and water until lumps disappear. Stir into raspberry mixture. Cook, while stirring, until sauce thickens and is clear. Remove crêpes from oven. Place on individual plates. Spoon sauce over each serving. Serves 8.

Apple Crêpes Normandy

These crêpes are a specialty of my mother's. Serve them with warm maple syrup or sour cream and brown sugar. Sautéed ham slices are a nice accompaniment, too.

3 cups applesauce
1 tsp. cinnamon
2 tbs. warmed brandy or hot water
1/2 cup raisins
1/2 cup chopped walnuts or pecans

16 Basic Crêpes (p. 112) or Sweet
    Crêpes (p. 115)
For serving:
hot maple syrup OR 1 cup sour cream
    AND 1 cup firmly packed brown
    sugar

Mix applesauce with cinnamon. In a small bowl, pour brandy over raisins. Let stand 1/2 hour. Add raisin-brandy mixture and walnuts to applesauce. Place a tablespoonful of the filling on each crêpe and roll. Place crêpes, seam side down, in a buttered, ovenproof dish. May be covered and refrigerated or frozen at this point. (Refrigerate for up to 1 day in advance. Freeze for up to 2 months.) Bake at 375°F. for 20 minutes, or until heated through and piping hot. If frozen, allow 10 to 15 minutes additional baking time. Serve with maple syrup or sour cream and brown sugar. Serves 6 to 8.

Marlene's Day-Before French Toast

6 slices French or Italian style bread,
    cut on the diagonal into 3/4-inch
    thick slices
3 eggs
1 cup milk
3 tbs. sugar
1/4 tsp. salt
1/2 tsp. nutmeg
1 tsp. vanilla
3 tbs. melted butter

For serving (choose an assortment):
    powdered sugar
    syrup
    sour cream
    fresh berries
    preserves or jams
    frozen fruits, thawed

Arrange bread in a single layer in 9-inch square baking dish. Combine eggs, milk, sugar, salt and vanilla. Beat until smooth. Pour over bread. Turn slices to coat evenly. Cover and refrigerate overnight. To cook, melt butter in skillet or on a grill. Remove bread slices from egg mixture. Sautée in heated pan until golden, about 5 minutes on each side. Sprinkle with powdered sugar. Serve with one suggested topping. Serves 4.

Ham and Shrimp Gâteau

In this recipe, Basic Crêpes are stacked with a rich and savory ham and shrimp sauce. Another dish to assemble ahead.

6 tbs. butter
1/4 cup finely sliced green onion
1/2 lb. fresh mushrooms, sliced
1 cup diced cooked ham
1 cup tiny shrimp
3 tbs. all-purpose flour
1 can (10 ozs.) chicken broth, undiluted

1/4 cup cream
1/4 tsp. dry mustard
1/2 tsp. EACH salt and white pepper
2 tbs. dry white wine
1 cup grated Parmesan OR Swiss cheese
8 large crêpes, prepared according to
    Basic Recipe, page 112

Melt 3 tablespoons of the butter in a heavy skillet over medium heat. Sauté green onion and mushrooms until tender. Add ham and shrimp. Stir in remaining butter until melted. Sprinkle with flour. Add chicken broth, cream, mustard, salt, pepper and wine. Cook until thick and bubbly. Add half of the cheese. Stir until melted. To assemble Gâteau, lightly butter a large ovenproof shallow casserole or platter. Place a crêpe in the center, cover with a layer of the sauce. Repeat layers until all the sauce and crêpes have been

120

used. Sprinkle top with remaining cheese. May be covered and refrigerated overnight at this point. Bake Gâteau at 375°F. for 30 to 40 minutes, or until Gâteau is piping hot and top is browned. Cut into wedges to serve. Serves 4 to 6.

Crispy French Toast

Cornflakes make a crispy crust; serve with a tangy sour cream sauce. Bacon or sausage makes a nice side dish.

1 cup evaporated milk
3 tbs. water
1 egg
1 tsp. vanilla
1 tbs. sugar
1/2 tsp. salt
1/2 tsp. cinnamon

10 slices day-old bread
2 cups cornflake crumbs
Strawberry Sour Cream Sauce:
1 pkg. (10 ozs.) frozen strawberries,
    thawed
1 cup sour cream
1/2 tsp. nutmeg
1/2 tsp. cinnamon

Combine evaporated milk, water, egg, vanilla, sugar, salt and cinnamon in a shallow dish. Beat well. Dip bread into this mixture and then into cornflake crumbs. Brown toast on both sides on a lightly buttered griddle over medium-high heat. While French Toast is browning prepare Strawberry Sour Cream Sauce. Stir all ingredients together in a small bowl. Spoon over hot toast. Serves 6.

Grandma's Oatmeal Hotcakes

My tiny little white-haired Grandma has got to be one of the greatest cooks in the world. In one of her notes she said: "I halve it for me. Use 2 eggs not 1 1/2! It keeps good in the refrigerator and will last me three mornings. Love, Grandma."

2 cups rolled oats
2 cups buttermilk
3 eggs, beaten
2 tbs. sugar
4 tbs. melted shortening

1/2 scant cup all-purpose flour
1 tsp. baking powder
1 tsp. baking soda
1 tsp. salt

Stir oatmeal and buttermilk together in a bowl. Cover and let stand on counter overnight. The next morning, add eggs, sugar and melted shortening. Stir well to combine. Sift flour, baking powder, soda and salt into oatmeal mixture. Stir until just combined. Cook on a lightly greased hot griddle until bubbles appear and underside is golden brown. Turn once. 12 hotcakes.

Sour Cream Pancakes

Sour cream makes these pancakes exceptionally light, crisp and tender. Try using warmed blueberry pie filling with a dash of cinnamon as a topping. They freeze well, wrapped individually in foil or plastic wrap. When reheating, allow them to thaw a minute or two before popping them into the toaster.

1 1/3 cups milk
1 cup sour cream
2 eggs
2 tbs. butter, melted
2 cups pancake or biscuit mix

Combine milk, sour cream, eggs and melted butter in a bowl. Mix thoroughly. Add pancake mix and stir just to combine. Mixture should be lumpy. Pour onto a hot, lightly greased pancake griddle or frying pan. Cook until bubbles appear and underside is golden brown. Turn once. Serve hot with lots of butter and warm syrup. Makes 30 medium-sized pancakes.

Dutch Babies

Almost everyone loves Dutch Babies for their antics. These big, puffy, popover like pancakes do all sorts of exciting things in the oven—bubble, pop, end up in marvelous shapes. Try using different sorts of pans for variety. Almost any baking pan with shallow sides can be used—pie plates, paella pans, ovenproof casseroles or skillets. Dutch Babies must be served immediately after leaving the oven, because they collapse within minutes. Toppings can be as simple as a sprinkling of powdered sugar and a squeeze of lemon juice. Also, try maple syrup, jams, sliced peaches and raspberries, strawberries and whipped cream, or warmed canned pie filling.

Serving:

Size	Butter	Eggs	EACH milk and flour	Pan Size
2 to 3	1/4 cup	3	3/4 cup	8-inch pie pan
3 to 4	1/3 cup	4	1 cup	9-inch square pan
4 to 5	1/2 cup	5	1 1/4 cup	10-inch pie pan or casserole
5 to 6	1/2 cup	6	1 1/2 cup	13 x 9-inch pan

Preheat oven to 425°F. Put butter in pan. Place pan in oven and melt butter. Watch closely so butter does not burn. Place eggs in the work bowl of food processor or blender container and whirl until just beaten. Add milk and flour and combine until mixture is just blended. Do not overmix, batter should be slightly lumpy. Pour batter into pan containing hot melted butter and return to oven. Bake for 20 to 25 minutes until puffed and golden.

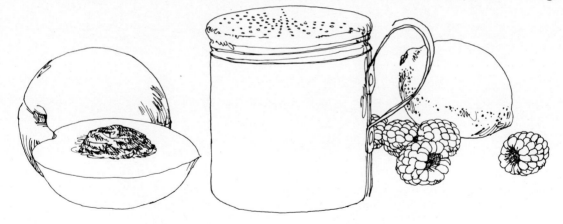

Coffee Cakes and Pastries

As the melodious slogan reminds us, "Nothing says lovin' like something from the oven." The aromas of freshly baked coffee cakes and pastries wafting through the air welcome your guests like a big hug and earn compliments galore.

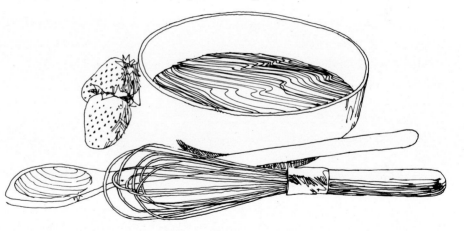

Jam-Filled Coffee Cake, p. 130

Jam-Filled Coffee Cake

The choice of filling is up to you for this quick and easy coffee cake. The shaping of the cake sounds complicated but isn't and the results are impressive.

Dough:
1 pkg. (3 ozs.) cream cheese
4 tbs. butter, softened
2 cups biscuit mix
1/3 cup milk
1/3 cup jam for filling (strawberry, peach, raspberry, apricot, or orange marmalade)

Glaze:
1 cup powdered sugar
2 tbs. milk or cream
1 tsp. vanilla
1/4 cup finely chopped walnuts (optional)

Cut cream cheese and butter into the biscuit mix until crumbly. Blend in milk. Stir to make smooth dough. Turn dough out onto lightly floured surface and knead 10 times. Pat or roll dough out on a sheet of floured waxed paper into 12 x 8-inch rectangle. Butter a cookie sheet. Lift up waxed paper and transfer dough onto prepared cookie sheet. Peel off waxed paper. With the tip of a table knife, very gently mark the dough lengthwise

130

into thirds. Spread the jam filling down the center portion. With a sharp knife, cut at one-inch intervals down each of the long sides of the dough, from the edge to the filling. Crisscross the dough strips over the filling, working from side to side (see illustration). Bake the coffee cake at 425°F. for 12 to 15 minutes or until golden. While coffee cake is baking, prepare glaze. Mix all glaze ingredients together in a small bowl. Drizzle over warm coffee cake; sprinkle with nuts, if desired. Cut into slices and serve. Makes 8 servings.

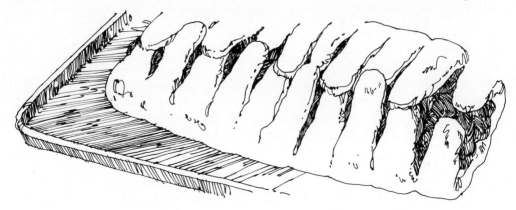

Crumbly Walnut Coffee Cake

Topping:
2 tbs. butter, softened
1/2 cup firmly packed brown sugar
1 tbs. all-purpose flour
1 tsp. cinnamon
1 cup coarsely chopped walnuts
    (whole if using processor)

Batter:
1 1/2 cups all-purpose flour
1/2 tsp. salt
2 tsp. baking powder
3/4 cup sugar
1/2 cup milk
2 eggs

Prepare topping first. Combine topping ingredients in a small bowl or in work bowl of a food processor. Process or mix until crumbly. Remove and set aside. Add flour, salt and baking powder to the work bowl or mixing bowl and blend briefly. Add sugar, milk and eggs to the flour mixture and combine just until moistened. Butter a 9-inch pie pan. Pour half of batter into pan, sprinkle with half of topping. Top with remaining batter. Sprinkle with rest of topping. Bake at 350°F. for 30 minutes, or until cake tests done. Cut in wedges and serve. Serves 6 to 8.

Lydia's Sour Cream Coffee Cake

1 1/2 cups butter, at room temperature
1 1/2 cups sugar
3 eggs
1 1/2 cups sour cream
1 1/2 tsp. vanilla
3 cups all-purpose flour

1 1/2 tsp. EACH baking powder and
    baking soda
1/4 tsp. salt
Filling:
3/4 cup firmly packed brown sugar
3/4 cup chopped walnuts
1 1/2 tsp. cinnamon

Generously butter a 10-inch angel food or bundt cake pan. Using an electric mixer, cream together butter and sugar until fluffy. Add eggs and sour cream. Beat for 2 minutes. Add vanilla. Sift together flour, baking powder, baking soda and salt. Add to creamed mixture and beat for 1 minute. In a small bowl, combine filling ingredients. Pour about a third of the batter into prepared pan. Sprinkle with half of the filling. Add another third of the batter and top with the remaining filling. Pour rest of batter over top. Bake at 325°F. for 1 hour, or until cake tests done. Let cool 15 to 20 minutes in pan before unmolding. Serves 12.

Cherry Pastry

This attractive looking pastry freezes well. Other fillings, such as apple, pineapple, peach or blueberry can be used. The lattice topping is prettier if you place it on the diagonal.

1 pkg. active dry yeast
1 tbs. sugar
3/4 cup warm water
3 cups all-purpose flour
3/4 cup butter, cut into 8 pieces
4 egg yolks
2 cans (21 ozs. each) cherry pie filling

Glaze:
3/4 cup powdered sugar
2 tbs. milk
1 tsp. almond extract

Combine yeast sugar and water in a large bowl or the work bowl of a food processor. Process or beat for a few seconds to combine. Cover and let sit for 10 minutes in a warm place. Add 1 cup flour, butter and egg yolks to the yeast mixture. Process or beat until well combined. Add remaining flour and process or beat until smooth. If you are not using a heavy-duty mixer, it may be necessary to knead in the remaining flour by hand.

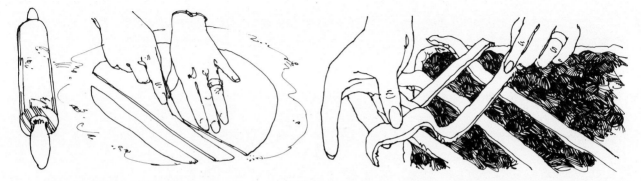

To assemble: Roll dough out on a lightly floured surface into a 15-inch square. Cut off and reserve a 5-inch strip of dough. Place the large rectangle of dough in a lightly buttered jelly roll pan, measuring 10 x 15 x 1-inch. Press edges of dough up the side of the pan to form a rim. Spread with pie filling. Cut remaining dough into 1-inch wide strips. Crisscross them over filling in a diagonal lattice pattern. Crimp edges. Cover and let rise in a warm place for 30 minutes. Bake at 350°F. for 15 to 20 minutes or until golden. Combine glaze ingredients in a small bowl. Drizzle on pastry while still warm. Cut into squares and serve. Makes 18 squares.

Oslo Kringler

This almond pastry is quite easy to prepare. It's been in Scandinavian families, including mine, for years. The only variation seems to be in the shaping of the dough, which differs from family to family. Some folks like it all in one piece, and others shape the Kringler into long narrow strips.

Crust:
1 cup all-purpose flour
1/2 cup butter
1 tbs. water

Topping:
1 cup water
1/2 cup butter
1 cup all-purpose flour
3 eggs
2 tsp. almond extract

Icing:
1 cup powdered sugar
1 tsp. vanilla
1 to 2 tbs. milk
1/2 cup sliced almonds (optional)

Prepare crust by cutting 1/2 cup butter into 1 cup flour until it resembles coarse cornmeal. Sprinkle with water. Stir to make a smooth dough. Using the back of a spoon, spread onto a buttered cookie sheet until crust measures 8 x 12 x 1/2 inches. Make topping by bringing water and butter to a boil over medium high heat. Add flour and stir vigorously until mixture pulls away from the side of the pan. Add eggs one at a time, stirring constantly. Stir in almond extract. Spread evenly over prepared crust. Bake at 375°F. for 45 minutes, or until lightly golden brown. Cool slightly. Combine powdered sugar, vanilla and milk in a small bowl until icing is thin enough to drizzle. Drizzle over warm Kringler. Sprinkle with the almonds. Cut into squares and serve warm. Makes 18 squares.

Almond Danish

These richly flaked pastries, filled with delicate almond butter cream, literally melt in your mouth.

1 cup ice-cold butter,
    cut into 1-inch cubes
3 cups all-purpose flour
2 pkgs. active dry yeast
1/4 cup warm water
1/4 cup PLUS 1 tsp. sugar
1/2 cup evaporated milk
2 eggs, room temperature
1 tsp. salt
paper cupcake liners

Butter Cream:
3/4 cup butter
1 1/4 cups powdered sugar
1/4 cup almond paste
2 tsp. vanilla
Almond Icing:
1 cup powdered sugar
2 tbs. milk
1/2 tsp. almond extract

Place butter and flour in large mixing bowl or work bowl of a food processor. Process or beat butter and flour together until butter is the size of kidney beans, no smaller. Refrigerate mixture while preparing yeast mixture. Combine yeast, water and 1 tsp. sugar.

138

Stir gently. Cover and let sit for 10 minutes in a warm oven to "proof" yeast. Add remaining sugar, evaporated milk, eggs and salt. Stir to blend. Pour this mixture over the butter and flour mixture, stir together until just blended. You should still have lumps of butter throughout. Cover and refrigerate dough for 4 hours or overnight.

To assemble pastries: Mix Butter Cream ingredients in a bowl until smooth and creamy. Set aside. Remove dough from refrigerator and divide in half. Return one half to the refrigerator. Roll remaining portion on a lightly floured surface into a 8 x 16-inch rectangle. Spread evenly with one half of Butter Cream. Roll up from the long side. Cut roll into sixteen 1-inch wide slices. Repeat with remaining dough and Butter Cream. Place each slice in a cupcake liner. Place pastries 1 inch apart on a baking sheet. Cover pastries and rise in warm place until doubled in volume, about 1 hour. Bake at 400°F. for 12 to 15 minutes, or until light golden brown. Prepare Almond Icing by mixing all ingredients together in a small bowl. While pastries are still warm, drizzle with the icing. Makes 32 pastries.

Brown Sugar Sticky Buns

This recipe makes a big batch and the rolls freeze very well. One time my sister-in-law Susie carried a frozen foil-wrapped package of these rolls from Pittsburg to the Caribbean in her suitcase, where we gobbled them for Christmas breakfast.

Dough:
1 pkg. dry yeast
1 cup milk, scalded (about 110°F.)
1/2 cup sugar
1 tsp. salt
2 eggs
1/2 cup melted shortening
4 1/2 cups all-purpose flour

Filling:
1/3 cup butter, softened
1 cup firmly packed brown sugar
2 tbs. cinnamon
1/4 cup finely chopped pecans (optional)
Topping:
1 cup butter
1 1/3 cups firmly packed brown sugar
4 tsp. light corn syrup

Place yeast in mixing bowl or food processor. Add milk and sugar. Process or beat until combined. Add salt, eggs, shortening and half of the flour. Process or beat until a smooth dough forms. Add remaining flour and combine. It may be necessary to knead in remaining flour by hand. Place dough in a buttered bowl, turning to coat the surface. Cover and let rise in a warm place until double, about 1 to 2 hours.

Meanwhile, prepare Topping. Melt butter in a small saucepan. Add brown sugar and corn syrup. Mix well. Bring to a rolling boil and take off heat immediately. Do NOT overcook. Pour topping into two 9 x 13-inch pans. Prepare buns. Punch dough down. Divide in half. Roll each piece out into a 9 x 18-inch rectangle. Spread with half of the butter for Filling; sprinkle with brown sugar, cinnamon and nuts, if desired. Roll up tightly from the long end. Repeat with other half of dough and Filling. Cut each roll into eighteen 1-inch slices. Place rolls in prepared pans. Cover and let rise in a warm place until doubled, about 1 hour. Bake at 375°F. for 20 to 30 minutes, or until golden. Remove from oven and turn immediately onto sheets of foil. Let cool a bit before serving or cool completely before wrapping for freezing. May be frozen for up to 2 months. Makes 3 dozen.

Cottage Cheese Croissants

These buttery little crescents are not nearly the trouble their namesakes are. They mix up in a matter of minutes. They complement egg dishes nicely.

1 cup butter, at room temperature
1 1/2 cups small curd cottage cheese
2 cups all-purpose flour

Glaze:
1 tbs. melted butter
1 tbs. cream or milk
1 cup powdered sugar
1 tsp. fresh lemon juice

Combine butter and cottage cheese in mixing bowl or work bowl of food processor. Beat or process until mixture is light and fluffy. Add flour. Mix until dough forms. Wrap dough tightly and refrigerate from 4 hours to overnight. Divide dough into thirds. Return 2 portions to refrigerator. Roll remainder into a 10-inch circle on a well floured board. Cut circle into 8 wedges. Roll each wedge into a crescent, beginning from wide edge. Repeat rolling, cutting and shaping process with remaining portions of dough. Place on lightly buttered cookie sheets, 2 inches apart. Bake at 350°F. for 45 minutes, or until golden brown. While croissants are baking, prepare Glaze. Combine first 3 ingredients in a small

142

mixing bowl. Stir well. Add enough lemon juice to make Glaze of drizzling consistency. Drizzle or brush on tops of croissants. Serve with assorted jams while still warm. Makes 24 croissants.

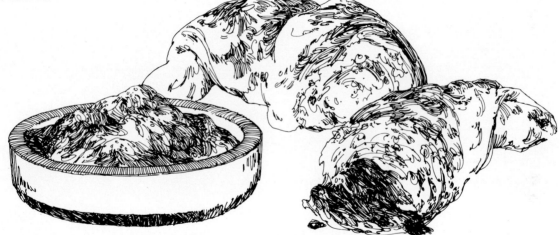

Sauces and Special Touches

When you want your meal to look as good as it tastes, turn to this chapter for some different ideas.

Why not make that special someone in your life feel extra special by preparing a cozy brunch for just the two of you? On a storming, wintery day, serve brunch on trays in front of a blazing fire. When the weather turns warmer, move outside. Serve brunch on a patio, deck or lawn. Groupings of potted or cut flowers will really brighten the occasion.

Guests at your next brunch will appreciate warmed guest towels at the end of the meal. Dip colorful fingertip towels into hot, scented water. Use a drop or two of your favorite cologne or scent extract. Wring them out tightly and wrap them in foil or a plastic bag. When you are ready to pass them around, reheat them briefly in a 250°F. oven or a microwave oven. Be sure not to put the plastic bag in an ordinary oven or the foil into the microwave.

Present food in unusual containers. For example, fruit compotes are striking served in large wine goblets.

A charming way to end a brunch is to let each guest flavor his own coffee. Provide plenty of it and a choice of mugs or cups and saucers. Set out whipped cream and an assortment of liqueurs, chocolate chips, tiny marshmallows and cinnamon sticks.

145

Raisin Sauce for Ham, p. 147
Spiced Jelly, p. 149

Basic Hollandaise

This classic sauce is easily made in a food processor or blender. Keep in mind that Hollandaise is served warm NOT hot. It can be kept warm in the top of a double boiler (over low heat) or in a thermos for several hours.

1/2 cup melted butter
3 egg yolks
1 to 2 tbs. lemon juice
dash of Tabasco sauce
1/2 tsp. EACH salt and white pepper

Cut butter into chunks. Melt in a small saucepan over medium heat. Watch carefully so it doesn't burn. Combine egg yolks, lemon juice and seasonings in a blender or food processor. With the motor running, slowly add the bubbling butter to the egg-yolk mixture. Makes 1 cup.

Raisin Sauce for Ham

Serve this special sauce along with your Easter ham and wait for the compliments.

1 cup raisins
1 1/4 cup orange juice
1/3 cup firmly packed brown sugar
1 1/2 tbs. cornstarch
1/4 tsp. EACH cinnamon and cloves
1/4 tsp. dry mustard
1 cup pecan halves (optional)

Combine raisins and orange juice in a saucepan. Cook over medium heat until raisins are plump, about 5 minutes. In a small bowl mix together brown sugar with cornstarch. Stir into raisin mixture. Add spices and cook, while stirring, until thickened. Add pecans, if desired. Serve hot sauce over ham. Makes 1 1/2 cups.

Rich Cheese Sauce

This versatile sauce can be combined with shrimp or crab and served on toasted English muffins. Or try adding some sautéed mushrooms and diced ham for use as a filling for crêpes. Leave out the cheese and substitute nutmeg for the mustard and you have a very good cream sauce.

1/4 cup butter
1/4 cup all-purpose flour
1 3/4 cups light cream or milk
1/2 tsp. salt
1/4 tsp. white pepper

1/4 tsp. dry mustard
1/2 cup grated cheese
    (Parmesan, Swiss or Cheddar)
2 egg yolks, lightly beaten

Melt butter in a small saucepan. Whisk in flour and cook for several minutes, stirring constantly. Gradually add cream, stirring constantly until thickened. Add salt, pepper and dry mustard. Remove pan from heat and stir in cheese. Whisk a small amount of sauce into egg yolks. Add egg yolk mixture to rest of sauce. Makes 2 cups.

Spiced Jelly

This jelly is great over baked ham. Also try topping an eight-ounce cube of cream cheese with it. Serve a variety of crackers on the side. It makes a lovely gift at Christmas time, placed in a pretty glass jar and dressed up with a ribbon and the recipe.

1 jar (18 ozs.) apple jelly
1 jar (18 ozs.) peach jam OR apricot-pineapple jam
1/4 cup prepared horseradish
1 tbs. dry mustard
1 tbs. ground white pepper

Mix all ingredients together until smooth. Cover and store in the refrigerator. Makes 5 cups.

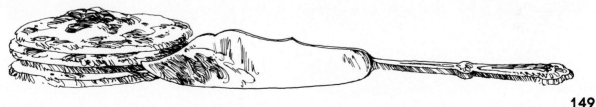

Salads

We don't usually think of salad as a breakfast dish, but for Brunch it can be used as a first course or served along with the meal just as at any other time of day. Or it can be a fruit salad, offered as a dessert. Colorful salads with attractive garnishes add a lot to the look of your table, too.

Be sure to keep the rest of your menu in mind when planning a salad to complement your brunch. Vegetable salads go nicely with the egg dishes and casseroles. Fruit salads should be served when the appetizer, main dish or dessert does not contain fruit.

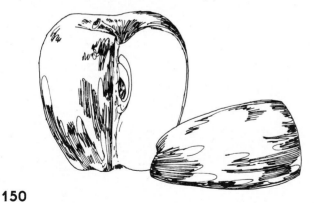

Raspberry Lemonade Mold

If you prepare this recipe in a ring mold, fill the center with frosted grapes or fresh blueberries.

1 pkg. (10 ozs.) frozen raspberries, thawed
1 pkg. (6 ozs.) raspberry gelatin
2 cups boiling water
1 pint vanilla ice cream, softened
1 can (6 ozs.) frozen pink lemonade concentrate
1/4 cup chopped pecans OR walnuts

Drain raspberries and reserve syrup. Dissolve gelatin in boiling water. Stir in softened ice cream. Add reserved raspberry syrup and lemonade concentrate, blending until smooth. Chill until partially set. Fold in raspberries and pecans. Pour into a 6-cup ring mold or other attractive mold. Chill several hours or overnight until set. Serves 8.

Pretzel Salad

Crust:
2 1/2 cups coarsely crushed pretzels
3/4 cup butter, melted
3 tbs. sugar

Filling:
1 pkg. (8 ozs.) cream cheese
1 envelope Dream Whip topping mix, dry
1 cup sugar

Topping:
1 pkg. (6 ozs.) strawberry Jello
2 cups boiling water
2 pkgs. (10 ozs. each) frozen
    strawberries, thawed

Combine all crust ingredients in mixing bowl or food processor. Process or mix by hand until well mixed. Pat into a 13 x 9 x 2-inch pan. Bake at 375°F. for 10 minutes. Cool. Combine filling ingredients in mixing bowl or food processor. Process or beat until mixture is light and fluffy. Spread evenly over cooled crust. Make topping. In a bowl, stir together Jello and boiling water until dissolved. Add berries and chill until partially set. Pour over cream-cheese mixture. Chill for several hours or overnight before serving. Cut into squares and serve. Serves 12.

Melon, Cucumber and Tomato Salad

An unusual combination of succulent textures, this salad is particularly tasty and refreshing. It's another recipe from Cordon Bleu, where it was served before a dinner that featured trout. Peeling tomatoes is simple and it makes an appreciable difference in many dishes. Take a minute or two to master the technique, you'll be glad you did.

1 honeydew melon
1 lb. fresh tomatoes
1 English cucumber
Mint Dressing:
2 tbs. red wine vinegar
6 tbs. salad oil

1 tbs. chopped parsley
2 tsp. chopped chives
2 tsp. chopped mint
2 tsp. sugar
1 tsp. salt
1/2 tsp. pepper

Cut melon into 1-inch cubes or make melon balls with a melon baller. Place melon in a large bowl. To peel tomatoes, bring a pan of water to a boil. Dip each tomato into the boiling water, count to 8 and remove. This allows you to slip the skin off the tomato almost effortlessly. Repeat with remaining tomatoes. Quarter the tomatoes and remove and discard seed and juice. Cut wedges in half again. Add to melon. Peel cucumber. Cut

154

into 1-inch cubes. Combine with the melon and tomatoes. Combine all dressing ingredients in a food processor or blender. Process or blend until combined. Pour over salad and toss gently to distribute dressing evenly. Cover and refrigerate for several hours before serving. Mixture should be icy cold. Serves 8.

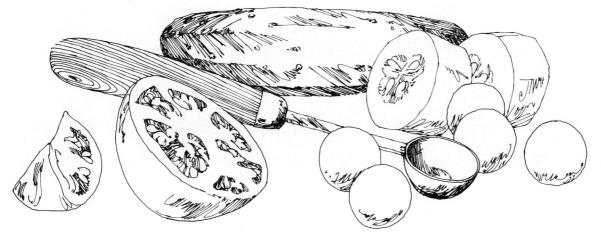

Marinated Mushroom Salad

Serve this delicately flavored salad on butter lettuce leaves and garnish with crumbled bacon.

1 lb. fresh mushrooms, sliced
4 green onions, sliced
Dressing:
2/3 cup olive oil
1/4 cup fresh lemon juice
1 tsp. Worcestershire sauce

1/2 tsp. dry mustard
1/2 tsp. salt
1/4 tsp. pepper
butter lettuce leaves (garnish)
crisp, crumbled bacon (garnish)

Place mushrooms and onions in a glass bowl. Combine dressing ingredients in a blender or food processor. Process or blend until well mixed. Pour over mushrooms and onions. Toss gently to combine. Cover and refrigerate for several hours or overnight. To serve, mound mixture on lettuce leaf and garnish with bacon. Serves 6.

Hint: At the Cordon Bleu we learned to toss gently by using the handles of forks or spoons, in order not to bruise the ingredients.

Hot Seafood Salad

Why not plan a salad brunch? Seafood salad makes a wonderful main dish, served with a fresh fruit salad and a tossed green salad as accompaniments. Offer hot French bread topped with garlic butter, herbs and cheese. A nice dessert would be cookies.

2 3/4 cups uncooked sea shell macaroni
1 can (approximately 7 ozs.) crab
1 can (approximately 7 ozs.) shrimp
1 can (approximately 7 ozs.) tuna
1 medium green pepper, chopped

2 hard-cooked eggs, coarsely chopped
1 pint Miracle Whip brand salad dressing
2 tbs. dry bread crumbs
2 tbs. melted butter
paprika

Cook macaroni in boiling salted water until just tender. Cool. Drain and pick over crab, shrimp and tuna. In a large bowl, combine cooled macaroni, crab, shrimp, tuna, green pepper, eggs and Miracle Whip. Place mixture in an ovenproof casserole. Cover and refrigerate for several hours or overnight. Heat oven to 475°F. Sprinkle casserole with bread crumbs, drizzle with butter and top with a dash of paprika. Bake for only 15 minutes. Serves 6 to 8.

Five-Cup Salad

Here's a traditional favorite. Serve it along with an egg casserole, ham or sausage and hot muffins. A sparkling fruit drink could be served before the meal. This salad tastes better if made a day ahead.

1 cup mandarin oranges, drained
1 cup pineapple cubes, drained
1 cup miniature marshmallows
1 cup shredded coconut
1 cup sour cream
Maraschino cherries, optional

Combine all ingredients and chill. Garnish with cherries, if you like. Serves 6 to 8.

Copper Pennies

2 lbs. carrots, peeled and sliced
1 large sweet white onion, peeled and
    sliced
1 green pepper, cored, seeded and
    sliced

Dressing:
1 can (10 ozs.) tomato soup, undiluted
3/4 cup cider vinegar
1/2 cup salad oil
1 tsp. mustard
1 tsp. Worcestershire sauce
1/2 tsp. salt
1/2 tsp. pepper

    Place carrots in a medium sized saucepan. Cover with water and bring to a boil. Cook until carrots are tender-crisp. Drain and cool. Separate onion slices into rings. Combine carrots, onions and green pepper slices in a bowl. Prepare dressing. Combine all ingredients in a saucepan and bring to a boil over medium heat, stirring occasionally. Pour dressing over prepared vegetables and cover. Refrigerate for at least 12 hours prior to serving. Keeps well for up to 2 weeks. Serves 8 to 10.

Desserts

The grand finale for any meal, these brunch desserts can run the gamut from simple fruit and cheese to the spectacular Rum Mousse Pie. Coffee cakes and pastries, as well as the recipes featured in the Fruit chapter, can also be used as desserts. Keep in mind your total menu. Naturally, you would not serve cake for dessert if coffee cake was served with the meal. Nor would you offer a fruit dessert if you served a fruit cup with the main course. Balance and contrast are the keys to selecting a brunch dessert. If your main course features a hearty entrée, select a dessert that is light yet satisfying. Dessert spectaculars can also be used as centerpieces. Any of the fancy coffees and a plate of cookies could be served as dessert.

Cakes are shown clockwise, starting at top: Sour Cream Poppy Seed Cake, p. 167; Butterscotch Pudding Cake, p. 170; Pumpkin Cake with Cream Cheese Icing, p. 166.

Cheese Ice Cream

This unusual dessert is not unlike cheesecake, but it's much lighter and tangier. It's a good recipe to have in your repertoire as it can be made ahead and frozen. Men love its taste and texture. This recipe was given to me years ago by a dear family friend who is a non-professional but wonderfully imaginative cook.

2 pkgs. (8 ozs. each) cream cheese
3/4 cup cottage cheese
1 cup sugar
4 eggs, separated

1 tsp. vanilla
1/2 cup heavy cream, whipped
2 cups vanilla wafer crumbs

Using an electric mixer, beat cream cheese and cottage cheese together until creamy. Add sugar and egg yolks and continue beating until light and fluffy. Stir in vanilla. Wash beaters thoroughly. In a separate bowl, beat egg whites until stiff. Fold cream and then egg whites into cheese mixture. Press about two third of the vanilla wafer crumbs into the bottom of a 9 x 13-inch dish. Pour in cheese mixture. Sprinkle with remaining vanilla wafers. Cover and freeze for 24 hours before serving. Makes 8 to 12 servings.

Schaum Torte

Schaum means "seafoam." This impressive dessert always makes guests exclaim that they can't possibly eat it all. Rest assured, they will! This light touch at the end of a meal leaves people satisfied but not stuffed.

12 egg whites, at room temperature
1 tsp. cream of tartar
2 cups sugar
1 tsp. vanilla
1 tsp. white vinegar

pinch of salt
1 pkg. (10 ozs.) frozen raspberries, thawed
1 cup whipping cream, whipped

Lightly butter bottom of a 10-inch spring-form pan. Sprinkle with 2 tsp. sugar. Beat egg whites with electric mixer, until foamy. Add cream of tartar. Slowly add all sugar, a spoonful at a time. Beat until very stiff peaks form. It is better to overbeat than underbeat. Add vanilla and vinegar and continue to beat for 2 more minutes. Gently spoon the mixture into the prepared pan. Bake at 275°F. for 2 hours. Turn off the oven and let set for several hours or overnight. To serve, drizzle thawed raspberries over the top. Spoon whipped cream over and cut into wedges. Serves 6 to 8.

Creamy Orange Fondue

This is delightful to serve when summer fruits are at their best. Plates of assorted fruits are lovely to look at, and leftovers can go into a nice salad. Dieters appreciate this dessert because they can just nibble on the fruits—IF they can resist the fondue!

1/4 cup butter
1/4 cup all-purpose flour
1 1/2 cups half-and-half
1/4 cup sugar
zest of one orange, finely grated
1 pkg. (8 ozs.) cream cheese, cubed
1/2 cup Grand Marnier liqueur

For Dipping:
Fresh fruits—strawberries, cherries, green seedless grapes, apricots, bananas, pears, apples, peaches
Canned fruits—mandarin oranges, pineapple chunks
Cubes of pound cake—chocolate is especially nice

In a heavy-bottomed saucepan, melt butter over medium heat. Whisk in flour. Slowly add half-and-half, stirring till smooth. Add sugar and orange zest. Stir in cubed cream cheese until melted. Add Grand Marnier. Cook until mixture is just bubbly. Pour into a fondue pot and keep warm over a votive candle. Use an assortment of fresh fruits for dipping. Be sure to have plenty of napkins on hand, as well as individual dessert plates. Serves 8 to 10.

Pumpkin Cake with Cream Cheese Icing

This rich cake is very easy to prepare, and it freezes well. For variety, try adding 1/2 cup of raisins or chopped pecans or walnuts to the cake batter.

2 cups sugar
4 eggs
1 cup salad oil
2 cups canned pumpkin
2 cups all-purpose flour
2 tsp. soda
2 tsp. cinnamon
1/2 tsp. salt

Cream Cheese Icing:
1/2 cup butter, softened
1 pkg. (8 ozs.) cream cheese
1 box (1 lb.) powdered sugar
2 tsp. vanilla

Combine all cake ingredients in a large mixing bowl. Beat with an electric mixer until thoroughly blended. Pour batter into a buttered and floured 13 x 9 x 2-inch pan. Bake at 350°F. for 35 to 40 minutes, or until cake tests done. Cool. Prepare Cream Cheese Icing. Combine icing ingredients in a mixing bowl. Beat with an electric mixer until smooth. Spread on cooled cake. Makes 10 to 12 servings.

Sour Cream Poppy Seed Cake

The light texture of this cake is heavenly!

1 pkg. (18.5 ozs.) white or yellow cake mix with pudding
1 cup sour cream
1/2 cup cream sherry
1/3 cup vegetable oil
3 eggs
1/4 cup poppy seed

Combine all ingredients in a large mixing bowl. Beat until smooth, about 2 minutes. Pour batter into a buttered bundt or tube cake pan. Bake at 350°F. for 35 to 45 minutes, or until cake tests done. Serves 12.

Mud Pie

This all-around favorite dessert can be served any time of day. If you serve it for brunch, make sure your main course is not too rich. Most of the ingredients can be purchased ready-made, so it's simply a matter of assembling the pie and garnishing with flair.

1/2 pkg. Nabisco chocolate wafers,
   crushed
1/4 cup melted butter
1 quart coffee ice cream, softened
1 1/2 cups rich fudge sauce

For garnish:
whipped cream
toasted almonds

Combine chocolate wafers and melted butter in a mixing bowl or a food processor. Process or stir until combined. Press into a buttered 9-inch pie plate. Cover with softened ice cream and return to the freezer until ice cream is firm. Spread with the fudge sauce and freeze overnight. To serve, cut into wedges and garnish with whipped cream and toasted almonds, if desired. Serves 8.

Hint: For a nice touch, serve wedges of pie on chilled dessert plates.

Butterscotch Pudding Cake

In this moist, rich cake mayonnaise is a surprise ingredient.

1 pkg. (18.5 ozs.) yellow cake mix
2 pkg. (3 ozs. each) butterscotch instant
    pudding mix
3 eggs
2 tbs. mayonnaise
1 1/2 cups water

Frosting:
1 pkg. (3 ozs.) cream cheese
1 cup firmly packed brown sugar
1/2 tsp. vanilla
2 containers (4 ozs. each) Cool Whip,
    thawed

Combine all cake ingredients in a large mixing bow. Beat with an electric mixer until smooth. Pour into a buttered 13 x 9 x 2-inch baking pan. Bake at 350°F. for 35 minutes, or until cake tests done. Cool cake. Prepare frosting. In a small bowl, mix cream cheese, brown sugar and vanilla until fluffy. Fold in Cool Whip. Spread frosting on cooled cake. Cut into squares and serve. Serves 12.

Rum Mousse Pie

This delectable pie recipe freezes well. If frozen, allow it to thaw overnight in the refrigerator the evening before your brunch. This recipe makes two pies; nice to have one tucked away in the freezer for another occasion.

6 egg yolks
1 cup sugar
1 pkg. unflavored gelatin
1/2 cup water

1/2 cup dark rum
1 pint whipping cream, whipped
two 8 or 9-inch graham cracker crusts
3 squares bitter chocolate, grated

Beat egg yolks and sugar with an electric mixer until very thick and lemon-colored. Dissolve gelatin with water in a small saucepan. Place gelatin over very low heat. Shake, don't stir, until gelatin melts completely. Watch carefully, as it burns easily. Fold gelatin into egg yolk mixture. Add rum. Fold whipped cream gently into egg mixture. Pour into crusts. Sprinkle with grated chocolate. Chill at least 6 hours before serving or freeze for longer storage. Cut into wedges to serve. Makes 12 servings.

Kentucky Butter Cake

If you like butter you'll love this cake. The hot butter sauce poured over the baked cake makes it exceptionally moist and delicious.

1 cup butter, at room temperature
2 cups sugar
4 eggs
1 cup buttermilk
2 tsp. vanilla
3 cups all-purpose flour
1 tsp. baking powder
1/2 tsp. baking soda
1/2 tsp. salt

Butter Sauce:
1 cup sugar
1/4 cup water
1/2 cup butter
1 tbs. vanilla

In a large mixing bowl, cream the butter and sugar with an electric mixer until fluffy. Beat eggs into the mixture one at a time, beating well after each addition. Stir in buttermilk and vanilla. Sift together flour, baking powder, baking soda and salt. Add to butter mixture, combining well. Pour into a buttered tube or bundt pan. Bake at 325°F for 60 to 65 minutes, or until cake tests done. Make Butter Sauce. Combine all sauce ingredients in a small saucepan and cook, stirring constantly until mixture is smooth and hot. Do NOT boil. Remove from heat and stir in vanilla. Pierce the entire surface of the cake with a fork. Pour hot Butter Sauce over cake. Let cool. Serves 12.

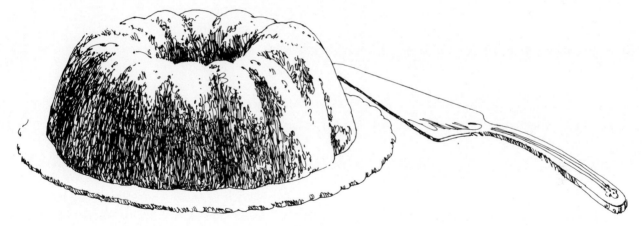

Blueberry Cream

This dessert has a wonderfully smooth texture, and the yogurt adds tang. It's nice to serve in August when blueberries are at their peak.

Crust:
1 1/4 cups graham cracker crumbs
1/4 cup sugar
6 tbs. melted butter

Filling:
1/2 cup sugar
1 envelope unflavored gelatin
3/4 cup cold water
1 cup sour cream
1 cup blueberry flavored yogurt
1 cup non-dairy whipped topping (Cool Whip)
1 cup blueberries

Combine graham cracker crumbs, sugar and butter. Reserve 1/4 cup of crumbs for topping. Press remaining crumbs into bottom of an 8-inch square baking dish. Bake at 375°F. for 8 minutes. Cool. Make filling. Combine sugar, gelatin and water in a small saucepan. Place mixture over medium heat, shaking the pan occasionally*, until gelatin

174

and sugar are completely dissolved.

Remove from heat and set aside. In a small bowl, combine sour cream and yogurt. Blend in gelatin mixture. Refrigerate until partially set. Stir in whipped topping. Fold in blueberries. If using canned or frozen blueberries, be sure to drain thoroughly. Spoon into prepared crust. Sprinkle with reserved crumbs. Refrigerate until set, about 2 hours. Cut into squares to serve. Serves 8.

*Hint: When I studied at the Cordon Bleu, we learned never to stir gelatin—it becomes stringy. Always shake gelatin to dissolve it.

Rheta's Chocolate Chip Bars

To me, cookies are just the right way to end a brunch—a touch of something sweet but not heavy.

1 1/2 cups all-purpose flour
1/2 cup butter
1/2 cup firmly packed brown sugar
1/4 tsp. salt
1 pkg. (6 ozs.) chocolate chips
2 eggs

1 cup firmly packed brown sugar
1 tsp. vanilla
2 tbs. all-purpose flour
1/4 tsp. salt
1/2 tsp. baking powder
1 1/2 cups flaked coconut

Combine first four ingredients and pat into the bottom of a lightly greased 13 x 9 x 2-inch baking pan. Bake at 375°F. for 20 minutes. Remove pan from oven and sprinkle chocolate chips evenly over crust. Return to oven for 1 minute to soften chips. Remove from the oven and spread chocolate evenly over the crust. Combine eggs, 1 cup brown sugar and vanilla. Stir in flour, salt and baking powder. Beat mixture until smooth. Stir in coconut. Spread mixture on top of chocolate. Bake for 14 minutes longer. Cool. Cut into bars. Makes 1 1/2 dozen.

Index